BASEBALL'S GOLDEN SEASON

The 1956 Major League Baseball Season, "Baseball's Greatest Year"

BASEBALL'S GOLDEN SEASON

The 1956 Major League Baseball Season
"Baseball's Greatest Year"

BILL LEATHERMAN

Alabaster Book Publishing
North Carolina

Published by Alabaster Book Publishing
P.O. Box 401
Kernersville, North Carolina 27285
www.alabasterbookpublishing.com

Book and cover design by
David Shaffer

Cover Photo by Bill Leatherman

Please address your comments to:
Bill Leatherman
wildbillleatherman@hotmail.com

First Edition

ISBN: 978-09815763-5-0

Acknowledgements

In the 1950's, The Sporting News was known as "The Baseball Paper of the World" and the Editor of this insightful baseball weekly, was J. G. Taylor Spink. The Sporting News was supported by numerous outstanding writers who contributed their articles on a weekly basis. Many of these were beat writers for specific teams, while others were independent freelance writers. All were outstanding contributors, both at the major league level and for the minor leagues. Many of the quotes and amusing stories from "Baseball's Golden Season" came from these writers and due credit is given.

Most of these beloved writers have passed on, but their outstanding works are remembered.

I am grateful to The Sporting News, and to the late J.G. Taylor Spink and the many contributing writers listed below. Without their works, "Baseball's Golden Season" would have not been possible.

J. G. Taylor Spink

Bob Addie
Lee Allen
Smith Barrier
Bob Bowie
Bob Broeg
Bill Bryson
Les Biederman
Don Bryant
Jimmy Burns
John Carmichael
Lou Chapman
Dan Daniel
Melvin Durslag
Jim Enright
Ben Foote
Art Gase
Sam Glassman
Frank Graham
L. H. Gregory
Howard Millard

Frank Haraway
John Hoffman
Hy Hurwitz
Max Kase
Joe King
Lloyd Larson
Fred Lieb
Carl Lundquist
Tom Meany
Ernest Mehl
Lou Miller
Ed McAuley
Roscoe McGowan
Don Oliver
Bill Rives
Harold Rosenthal
Oscar Ruhl
Tom Swope
Bob Wolf
Dick Young

Special thanks to my daughter-in-law, Michelle Leatherman who provided numerous helpful suggestions as I went along, and corrected a considerable number of my errors.

For all my family members who love baseball,
and for those who don't.

EVERYTHING ELSE YOU GROW OUT OF,
BUT YOU NEVER RECOVER FROM CHILDHOOD

The writing of "Baseball's Golden Season" brought back childhood memories for me and my friends who lived these special baseball moments together. Growing up in the Belmont section of Charlottesville, Virginia, in the shadow of Thomas Jefferson's Monticello, our friendships began in elementary school, much of it due to sports, baseball cards and our favorite teams. We were neighbors, friends, classmates and teammates. Many of our baseball companions have passed on, but special friends Paul Blincoe, Don Bourne, Allen Carver, Connie Crenshaw, Bill Lynch and Tommy Williams have continued our friendships for well over 60 years.

We each had our favorite teams which we followed so diligently from Opening Day to the World Series, all the while looking for the elusive baseball cards of Mickey Mantle, Stan Musial, Ted Williams and the other popular players of our time. Whether it was the Cardinals, Dodgers, Giants, Orioles, Senators or Yankees, we each had incredible loyalty to our own favorite team.

Our group is especially proud of our friend, Bill Lynch who has shared his own good fortune with so many, and has spent a lifetime helping others in and around Charlottesville. On October 11, 1951, the first time I ever skipped school (at eleven years old) was at the Lynch residence to see the Dodgers defeat the Giants 10-0 in a NL Playoff Game.

Table of Contents

Page

PREFACE

The summer of 1956 was the best of times! Our hometown of Charlottesville, Virginia was no different than any other city across the United States.

As sixteen year old baseball enthusiasts we lived and enjoyed a much more simple life than is afforded the youth of today. It was a time in our country when there was no knowledge of drugs to pique the interests of young people, no electronic gadgets to waste our youthful time, just a few channels on black and white twelve-inch televisions to help soothe away our downtime.

We were graduates of Little League Baseball some years earlier and a few of us were continuing to play in the area's fledgling American Legion Baseball program.

The greatest baseball season ever would begin on April 17, 1956. Just as in previous years when spring and baseball rolled around, we would visit our neighborhood grocery store near Belmont Park where for many years we boarded the morning school bus. The neighborhood grocery was located very near the bus stop, where I was certain to arrive early, so I could spend my lunch money on baseball cards.

The Topps and Bowman cards represented the greatest bargain in America, one penny for a pack of cards; which included one card and a large flat piece of bubble gum with a wonderful aromatic flavor none of us will ever forget. We collected and traded cards, but never put our cards into the spokes of our bicycles, as we had far too much respect for our cherished collection.

During this delightful summer of my tenth grade school year, I was carrying both a morning (Richmond Times-Dispatch) and evening newspaper, (Richmond News Leader) as I delivered the news to residences, restaurants and motels around our city.

Both the city of Charlottesville and the surrounding county of Albemarle was abuzz knowing the award winning movie, Giant, was in-part being filmed locally. The first part of the movie was filmed in nearby Keswick, using the old railroad station there for the Maryland portion of the film.

The cast, that included Rock Hudson and James Dean, were staying at the upscale Town & Country Motel. Everyone was hoping to get a glimpse of the actors and especially the beautiful 23 year old actress, Elizabeth Taylor. Each evening as I delivered my newspapers to the Town & Country, I hoped to see some of the cast, but to no avail, it never happened.

Prior to the 1956 season I had only seen one Major League Baseball game in my lifetime, that being August 24, 1952, when our Little League coach took our entire team to Washington, D. C., to see the Senators and Indians play in a contest that lasted sixteen innings.

Several of my friends and I did travel to New York City via Trailways bus to see the Dodgers, Yankees, and Giants in their respective stadiums during the July 4 weekend. We also stopped by to see the Phillies play in old Connie Mack Stadium on the return home. Quite a trip for young baseball fans, unaccompanied by adults. Absolutely unheard of today.

Major League Baseball stadiums of today are pristine cathedrals, built as much for entertainment and fine dining, as for baseball. As one who would be considered more than just your average baseball fan, I have attended the first game ever played at most of these newer stadiums, beginning with the opening of Oriole Park at Camden yards in 1992. Little did I know on that gorgeous day in Baltimore that some 30 years later, Camden Yards would be one of the older major league stadiums in existence today.

By 1956 many of the 16 aging baseball stadiums had seen their better days. I can attest as a youngster visiting Ebbets Field, the Polo Grounds, Yankee Stadium and especially Connie Mack Stadium, that the splinters in the bleachers of these hallowed parks can leave everlasting scars, yet provide pleasant lifetime memories for a sixteen year old, who had only dreamed of someday visiting these parks. Only Wrigley Field in Chicago and Fenway Park in Boston remain of the sixteen.

Beyond baseball, 1956 was one of the more remarkable years of the Twentieth Century. Rock and Roll was becoming a National phenomenon with the emergence of Elvis Presley and his songs like Hound Dog, Don't Be Cruel and Heartbreak Hotel. The latter two were the top tunes of the year.

A star, a legend, was "born" as Norma Jean Mortenson changed her name to Marilyn Monroe.

The live-virus oral Polio Vaccine was developed by Dr. Albert Sabin, to further help eradicate this horrible disease. Dr. Jonas Salk, just one year earlier had invented the vaccine for curing Polio.

Interstate highways were approved by Congress under the administration of President Dwight D. Eisenhower, who won a second term of office as the President of the United States.

The Pittsburgh Pirates and Kansas City Athletics canceled an exhibition baseball game in Birmingham, Alabama, due to a local ordinance than banned "negroes" from playing against whites.

On April 18, Umpire Ed Rommel became the first major league umpire ever to wear glasses.

Those alive today, will remember where they were when Don Larsen of the New York Yankees pitched the greatest game in baseball history. It just happened to be in game five of the 1956 World Series.

The Cincinnati Reds were called the Redlegs.

Hank Greenberg and Joe Cronin were elected to the Baseball Hall of Fame.

The 1956 Olympic Games were played in Melbourne, Australia. Team USA won the Basketball Gold Medal at a time when only amateurs could participate. The USA team was led by Bill Russell and K. C. Jones, teammates at the University of San Francisco, where they had won the NCAA Championship in both 1955 and '56.

Major League Baseball was in its pre-expansion era, as there were only eight teams in each league, creating better rivalries. There was much less player specialization, therefore helping create "Baseball's Golden Season."

There were no playoff situations for second place or "Wild Card" teams. Only the true pennant winner in each league advanced to the World Series. There were no Designated Hitters, no names on the back of jerseys and protective batting helmets were not in vogue.

Many great players had returned from both World War II and the Korean War. Some served multiple military terms, thus shortening their careers as active baseball players.

More of the great names in baseball's history played during the 1956 season than at any other time. Most of these Hall of Famers and great gentlemen of the game are gone now, but many are still alive.

Since I started this writing, Frank Robinson ('56 NL Rookie of the Year), Don Newcombe (baseball's first ever Cy Young Award winner and National League MVP), Don Mossi and

Bob Friend have passed away.

This would be the final season for Phil Rizzuto, Jackie Robinson and Bob Feller as major league players.

The 1956 World Series was the last New York Series between the Dodgers and Yankees. The two have played 11 times, seven of those before the 1958 move by the Dodgers to Los Angeles.

Night baseball, the beginning of air travel and this newer invention called "television" were helping to rejuvenate baseball. There were no teams in the western part of the United States, as St. Louis was baseball's westernmost team. MLB was moving on from the pleasantries of travel by train to air travel.

Minor league baseball in the 1950's was in a constant struggle. Intriguing stories as to how minor league teams operated, many folded during mid-season, while others brought us successful stories. 1956 was a pivotal year for the minor leagues, as finally Major League Baseball realized it would have to filter and support these fledgling leagues. Some of our better quotes and stories came from the colorful, lower minor leagues.

There were many extraordinary personalities dominating baseball in 1956, thus a tremendous amount of amazing, interesting and amusing baseball stories and anecdotes to enhance "Baseball's Golden Season."

CHAPTER ONE

Cold Weather, Night Baseball and Aging Stadiums
(The Season Begins, April 17, 1956)

Opening Day, April 17, Baseball's Golden Season was about to begin.

As was the custom, the Cincinnati Redlegs were always given the earliest start time for Opening Day, as their honor for being baseball's oldest franchise. On this day, the Redlegs hosted the St. Louis Cardinals at Crosley Field and lost a thriller as Stan Musial hit a two run home run in the top of the ninth inning off Joe Nuxhall for a 4-2 Redbird victory in front of 32,095 fans.

The season opener for a determined New York Yankee squad that had remained mostly in tact from the previous season saw the Bronx Bombers defeat the Washington Senators in Griffith Stadium with a resounding 10-4 victory. Mickey Mantle hammered two long home runs off Senators ace Camilio Pascual. Mantle and Yogi Berra led the onslaught, as Berra also homered, driving in five runs with a perfect four for four. Don Larsen went the distance for the Yankees while allowing four home runs, three of them by a little known Senator outfielder, Karl Olson.

Home plate umpire, Ed Rommel made history in the Yankees vs. Senators opener, as he became the first umpire in MLB history to wear glasses during a game.

In the Senior Circuit, the Dodgers dropped an 8-6 decision to the Philadelphia Phillies and ace Robin Roberts, who went the distance before 24,236 at Ebbets Field. Roy Campanella and Junior Gilliam each homered for the Dodgers. Roberts, who was known for his impeccable control also gave up a lot of home runs in his career, but most were solo shots.

Over 39,000 fans at County Stadium in Milwaukee watched a brilliantly pitched opener as Braves hurler Lew Burdette blanked the Chicago Cubs 6-0 on a five hitter, while striking out six batters. Future Hall of Famer Hank Aaron homered for the Braves, who were beginning their third season in Milwaukee since relocating from Boston in 1953.

The largest Opening Day crowd was at Briggs Stadium in Detroit, where 40,506 fans turned out to see the Kansas City Athletics defeat the hometown Tigers 2-1. In that contest, Tommy LaSorda, who later would become a Hall of Fame manager, earned the only save of his pitching career, closing it out for the A's. The Tigers only run came on a home run by pitcher, Frank Lary.

The Chicago White Sox defeated the Cleveland Indians 2-1 in Comiskey Park, as lefty Billy Pierce bested the Indians Bob Lemon. In the shortest played contest of the day, the game was played in just two hours and five minutes (2:05).

Of the eight contests played on Opening Day, the longest game was the Yankees vs Senators slugfest which lasted two hours and thirty-eight minutes (2:38). Four games were played under two hours and twenty minutes (2:20). MLB today has great concern about the length of their contests perhaps they should take a look at the 1956 openers?

Ticket sales to Yankee games, both home and away are surging and in addition to the Yankee name, the name Mickey Mantle seems to be on everyone's lips.

Mantle now ranks as one of the greatest gate attractions in the history of the game, taking his place alongside Babe Ruth and Bob Feller. "I must add Mickey to Ruth and Feller," said American League president, Will Harridge. "The reaction our office has received to Mantle's homers, and the distance of his homers is positively stunning. I can't recall anything like it. Everywhere I went this morning, in the restaurant, in the elevator and in the barber shop it was Mantle, Mantle, Mantle."

Harridge said that Mickey's magnetism is as great as Ruth's and Feller's because fans exclaim, "Mantle is in town," just as they did for the Bambino and Rapid Robert.

"Mind you," Harridge went on, "they said Mantle first and the Yankees second. That's what they used to say when Ruth and Feller were in their prime."

On an early season trip to Chicago the "I-shook-the-hand-of-Mickey Mantle club" enrolled its largest membership ever. The game was delayed time and again in the late innings as youngsters swarmed on the field in ever-increasing numbers to greet Mantle as he took his position in center field.

Ushers and police sought to keep up but nabbed only a few of the playful offenders, and the worst punishment for any was banishment from the park. The situation was worse in the ninth inning, when, by accurate count, 20 kids, including at least one girl, were on the field.

Adult fans had a role in the wild afternoon of misbehavior, too. One threw a paper container of beer into the Yankee dugout; another was arrested on a charge of biting an usher's arm and hundreds were among the celebrants who showered paper and trash on the playing field.

Nearby police headquarters received complaints from 15

fans who reported their parked cars ransacked outside the park and five men were arrested on charges of scalping tickets for the unbelievable cost of $15 each.

Yes, Mickey Mantle and the Yankees were in town!

Only 12,790 fans were present at the Polo Grounds for the New York Giants home opener as the New Yorkers defeated the Pittsburgh Pirates 4-3. Johnny Antonelli, the Giants winning hurler homered to help his own cause. Dale Long of the Pirates slammed two home runs in a losing effort. Just a few weeks later, beginning on May 19 and ending on May 28, the left-handed Buc first baseman would homer in eight consecutive games, setting a major league record that still stands today. Years later, Don Mattingly and Ken Griffey, Jr., tied the record as each had eight consecutive games with home runs. The record still stands today. When Long's streak ended he was batting .411 with 14 home runs. He tailed off later in the season and ended with a .263 average, hitting 27 homers and had 91 RBI.

Two years later, while playing for the Chicago Cubs, Dale Long became one of the very few left-handed catchers in MLB history, as he caught several innings in two games for the Cubs using a first baseman's mitt.

The amount of time it took to play games in '56 were considerably less than MLB games of today and they still only play nine innings! There are many opinions about how to shorten the length of major league games today, but the between innings time allocated for television commercials which were not so prevalent in Baseball's Golden Season obviously add to the length of games. The dollar talks!

Without the excitement of Opening Day, the midweek games that followed on Wednesday and Thursday saw some very small crowds as the weather was not ideal in the spring of 1956. Only 5,369 fans were in attendance at Comiskey Park in Chicago to see Sox hurler Jack Harshman defeat the Indians Herb Score in a classic duel 2-1. Each pitcher allowed only two hits, and the exciting lefty Score struck out 10 would be White Sox batters. He went on to have a fabulous season for the Indians, posting a 20-9 record while striking out 263 American League batters. Herb Score was destined to be the lefty version of Bob Feller, but on May 7, 1957, just one year later, he was hit in the eye by a line drive off the bat of the Yankees Gil McDougal, completely derailing his projected Hall of Fame career. Herb Score remained in baseball as he served as the Indians broadcaster for many years before his passing.

Attendance at the Polo Grounds in recent years had been declining drastically, and day two of the new season was no exception as the hometown Giants defeated the Pirates 5-4 before only 2,493 fans.

The numerous intentional bases on balls given to Ted Williams as the season began resulted in his only swinging the bat one time in a total of three plate appearances in the Red Sox contest against the Orioles. He singled in the fifth inning to drive in two Red Sox runners, triggering a six run fifth inning as the BoSox defeated the Orioles 8-4, behind the complete game pitching of Bob Porterfield.

The first extra-inning games of the season were on day three, with the Dodgers defeating the Phillies in 10 innings, in a contest played at Roosevelt Stadium in Jersey City, New Jersey. Dodger owner Walter O'Malley was in search of a new stadium to replace aging Ebbets Field, and he contracted to play seven home dates during the season in New Jersey in hopes of making the public and Brooklyn city council members aware, that if a new stadium was not in the works, then the beloved Dodgers will be leaving Brooklyn. During the season, the crowds at Roosevelt Stadium were similar to those of Ebbets Field. On this day, the first game played in Jersey City, there were 12, 214 fans in attendance.

The Brooklyn (Jersey) Dodgers were victorious over the Philadelphia Phillies by the score of 5-4, rallying for two runs in the bottom of the tenth inning, after the Phils had scored one in the top half to take the lead.

The Dodgers Carl Erskine and Murry Dickson of the Phillies both went nine innings. Brooklyn relief specialist, Clem Labine worked the top half of the tenth and gave up a run, but eventually was the winning pitcher as the Dodgers won it, compliments of the two run rally in their bottom half of the tenth. Don Zimmer, who was pinch-running, scored the winning run on a sacrifice fly by Rube Walker.

In another extra-inning affair the hometown Cincinnati Redlegs defeated the St. Louis Cardinals 10-9 in a slugfest. Only 2,438 were in attendance at Crosley Field on a cold afternoon to see the Redlegs rally in a similar fashion to the Dodgers, edging the Cardinals in the bottom of the tenth.

Stan Musial and Cards catcher Bill Sarni both homered for the Redbirds, with Sarni hitting his first and second homer of the young season. Ted Kluszewski, Wally Post and Smokey Burgess homered for the Redlegs.

Brooks Lawrence working in relief in the top of the tenth faced only two batters to earn the win. He struck out both with runners on base, after the Cardinals had scored the go ahead run and watched as his teammates rallied for the win.

Wally Post, who had homered earlier, hit a two out single, scoring Johnny Temple and Kluszewski with the tying and winning runs.

In this pre-expansion era there were a couple things that stood out to this author. I looked at numerous box scores, particularly in the first week or so of the season. Attendance was much more difficult financially for fans, as well as the availability for travel to weekday games, which were almost exclusively played in the afternoons. Attendance at those weekday games was very low, as many of the games drew only 2,000 or less fans. The records also indicate that the spring of 1956 was very cold with a lot of precipitation, especially in April, which forced many postponements.

There were a tremendous number of early season route going performances by pitchers, especially the more established veterans. An astonishing number of hurlers had excellent early season success, but the one thing that stood out is that each of these pitchers had very few strikeouts. The following is a list of pitchers in the first week or ten days of the season that had very successful outings, yet not one of them struck out more than SIX batters in any single contest. Names like; Billy Pierce, Robin Roberts, Roger Craig, Early Wynn, Bob Friend, Vern Law, Mike Garcia, Bobby Shantz, Bob Lemon, Frank Lary, Brooks Lawrence, Whitey Ford, Carl Erskine and Don Larsen were all obviously pitching to contact, thus, getting numerous ground ball outs, instead of strikeouts. This is evidenced by an average of 12 to 14 putouts by first basemen, whereas, currently with launch angle hitters there are many more putouts credited to catchers, due to the high propensity of strikeouts.

Even those hurlers recognized as the more proficient strikeout artists like Herb Score, Johnny Antonelli, Sam Jones, Vinegar Bend Mizell and Don Newcombe, were mostly striking out only seven or eight batters per nine innings as the season moved forward.

More than just a few of these pitchers are Hall of Famers, most had long and successful careers in MLB, which adds to the theory that pitchers in the pre-expansion era had far less arm injuries, surgeries, etc., than the pitchers of today, many who are throwing each and every pitch with maximum effort.

The legends of baseball continue to make wonderful baseball stories. One fan dredged up an interesting Ty Cobb-Walter Johnson story from many years back. When the great fireballer, Johnson was breaking into the game with Washington, the fiery Georgian (Cobb) warned him that he intended to beat out any bunt he laid down and heaven help the pitcher who got in his way on the way to first base. The gentlemanly Johnson nodded that he understood, said: "I feel it is only fair to let you know that the control of my fast ball might be a little off today." It stopped Cobb. (Oscar Ruhl)

After week one the powerful Yankees had stormed off to a 5-1 start. After taking two of three from the Senators, they opened at home by pounding the Red Sox in three straight games. Mickey Mantle had two more home runs, giving him four after the first week of the season, in his pursuit of the Triple Crown. The Yankees never looked back, as they maintained an edge over the White Sox and Indians early on with outstanding starting pitching. Whitey Ford and newcomers Johnny Kucks and Tom Sturdivant all were outstanding in the early going.

Word around baseball is that the most tantalizing knuckleball in the American League belongs to Mickey Mantle, while Gil Hodges has the best flutter pitch in the National League.

In the National League after week one, the Milwaukee Braves found themselves atop the standings with a 4-2 record. The Braves bolted out to a 3-0 mark behind consecutive outstanding pitching performances from Lew Burdette, Bob Buhl and Warren Spahn.

After, Burdette shut out the Chicago Cubs 6-0, behind home runs from Hank Aaron and Joe Adcock, Buhl followed Burdette's masterpiece with a gem of his own, a 3-1 win over the Cubbies. Game three saw Spahn defeat the Cardinals in St. Louis 5-4, as Eddie Mathews hammered two home runs.

Umpire Jocko Conlan says he can't remember having called a strike against Hank Aaron for more than half the season last year. "Aaron just won't let a good one go by, those wrists are so quick, if the ball is in the zone he attacks it."

Just 2,778 witnessed the Senators get their first win on day two of the season, a 3-2 victory over the Yankees at Griffith Stadium.

Kansas City earned a 4-1 win over the Detroit Tigers in Briggs Stadium, but it was only witnessed by 4,009 fans.

On Friday, April 20, Dodger right-hander Roger Craig

hurled a four-hitter to lead the Bums to a 5-0 win over the Pirates, as 23,357 witnessed the game on a sunny day in Forbes Field. Junior Gilliam had two hits for the Dodgers including a third inning two run homer that provided all the run support Craig would need on this day.

The season's first weekend action saw the Kansas City A's belt 20 hits off five Chicago White Sox pitchers in-route to a 15-1 thumping of the Pale Hose, all without benefit of a home run. Art Ditmar threw a one-hitter at the visitors, while striking out just three batters. Despite all the base hits, and pitching changes, the contest was played in only two hours and twenty minutes (2:20).

After a 0-3 start the Detroit Tigers picked up their first win of the season, defeating the Cleveland Indians 7-6, before 4,224 fans in spacious Cleveland Stadium. The Tigers drove Indian starter Mike Garcia from the game with a four run rally in the third inning. Detroit held a 6-0 lead after three innings and held on for the win.

Bob Friend of the Pirates matched Roger Craig's performance from the previous day, by holding the Dodgers to three hits, for his first victory of the season. Friend walked two and fanned three in leading the Bucs to the 3-1 win.

Frank Thomas and Dale Long each hit their third homer of the season, while Long had 18 putouts at first base, as the Pirate infield played outstanding defense behind Friend's efforts.

"They never throw at the right guy," said George Kell of the Orioles, commenting but not complaining about the number of times he has been flattened by pitchers already in the young season. "The fellow in front of me hits a home run, so I'm the fellow who has to scramble for his life on the next pitch, invariably head-high, fast and inside."

"From my standpoint," continued Kell, "it makes me a tougher hitter. When I get up off the ground I'm more determined than ever to get a hit."

Legend has it that knockdown pitches don't affect the good hitters. In fact, it makes better hitters of them because you're waking them up. It does disturb the fellows who are a little plate shy.

Johnny Rigney, who is vice president of the Chicago White Sox was an accomplished pitcher in his day, said, "I remember years ago I got knocked out against the Yankees and Jack Hallett went in to relieve me. Jimmy Dykes, managing us then, told him to knock some of them down. The first fellow Hallett faced was Joe DiMaggio. He threw behind Joe's head. On the next pitch Joe tripled."

"DiMaggio saw me and Hallett in the runway the next day," Rigney continued, "and said to me, without even looking at Hallett, 'I don't mind it when good pitchers throw at me, it's part of the game, but I don't like those bush leaguers trying it.' Hallett simply had made DiMaggio more determined to get a hit."

Horace Stoneham, the owner of the New York Giants felt that the Giants glory days in the Polo Grounds were a thing of the past and attendance numbers backed up his prognostications. Just 1,922 patrons found their way through the turnstiles on Thursday of Opening Week as the Pirates beat the Giants 3-2. There were other games during week one with low attendance, some were night games played in very "unlike and unfair baseball conditions."

The St. Louis Cardinals were somewhat of pioneers in ushering night games into Major League Baseball, as the St. Louis weather was more conducive to night baseball. The Redbirds were not only MLB's most western team, but they were also its southernmost team.

On Wednesday, April 25, the Cardinals defeated the Chicago Cubs 6-0 in another early season night game at Busch Stadium behind a two-hitter from lefty Harvey Haddix. Nicknamed "The Kitten" in reference to his Cardinal predecessor, lefty Harry "The Cat" Brecheen, Haddix struck out three and walked five in going the route for his first win of the season.

Baseball lore remembers Harvey Haddix as the man who just three years later, pitched quite possibly the greatest game ever, when on May 26, 1959 on a gray miserable night in Milwaukee, he hurled 12 perfect innings only to lose 1-0 in the thirteenth. Pitching for the visiting Pirates, Haddix saw his masterpiece crumble when the Braves' Felix Mantilla reached on an error by Pirates third baseman, Don Hoak. Eddie Mathews sacrificed Mantilla to second and Hank Aaron received an intentional pass. Joe Adcock then blasted a home run, ending the no-hitter and the game. However, in the confusion, Aaron left the infield, cutting across the diamond and was passed by Adcock for the second out and a 2-0 Braves win. The home run was later changed to a double, only Mantilla's run counted and the Braves won by a 1-0 score.

Years later, a baseball ruling change deprived Haddix of his perfect game. Still credited with a no-hitter, "The Kitten" was not upset, he stated: "It's o.k., I know what I did."

The hometown Cardinals batting against flame thrower, Sam Jones scored all the runs they would need in the first inning. After a base on balls to Don Blasingame, Stan Musial doubled before Jones walked Ken Boyer. Wally Moon then doubled to give the Cards a 3-0 lead that they never relinquished on a pleasant spring evening in Busch Stadium.

Jackie Robinson's theft of home in the Dodgers' game with the Giants on April 25 was the twentieth of the Brooklyn star's Major League career, including one in the 1955 World Series. The theft was unusual in that Jackie stopped midway between third base and the plate and then resumed his sprint. "I stopped because I thought I'd be out if Jim Hearn went through with the motion I thought he was using," explained Robinson. "He was bringing his hands up and I figured he was ready to go into the pitch. But then he brought his hands down and I went for the plate because I knew he'd have to bring his hands up again before he could throw."

Traditional doubleheaders are now mostly a thing of the past, but in the 1950's they were prevalent, especially on Sunday afternoons. On Sunday, April 29 there were six doubleheaders scheduled in MLB, five of them were played and the rained out Cardinals vs. Braves double-dip was rescheduled on Monday.

Enthusiasm of the fans in around Pittsburgh for the Pirates continues sky-high. Although Dale Long was still the key man in the attack and continuing to draw the headlines, Roberto Clemente was inching closer and closer to being the Buccos leading hitter.

Clemente, the 21-year-old Puerto Rican whom the Pirates drafted from the Dodger farm at Montreal two years ago for only $4,000, because he was a bonus player, is proving one of the best investments the Pittsburghers ever made.

Clemente, only in his second season in the major leagues has all the tools for greatness. He hits line drives, runs with the best, has a tremendous arm and can catch anything within reach.

Coach Clyde Sukeforth is credited with finding Clemente for the Bucs organization. Sukeforth was on a routine scouting assignment two years ago in Richmond, Virginia looking at Joe Black who belonged to the Dodgers and was playing for Montreal. "I saw Clemente and forgot all about Black," Sukey relates. "I got to the park in time to see Clemente making some throws from the outfield and I couldn't take my eyes off him. Later, I saw him bat and I really liked his swing."

"I started asking questions and found he was a bonus player and eligible for the draft. Since the Pirates had first choice, I knew this would be our man."

Leo Durocher, who had a 24 year major league managerial career once told a group of sportswriters his version of how Clemente landed with the Dodgers, instead of the Giants.

"We knew the boy in high school," Durocher related one day at the Polo Grounds, "but we didn't want to make him a bonus player. We felt he'd be better off if he remained in the minors. When the Dodgers heard we were after him, they got into the act."

"The Braves also bid for him, but the Dodgers felt if we got Clemente to pair up with Willie Mays, that would be too much competition. So they gave him a $10,000 bonus and sent him to Montreal, realizing they'd lose him in the draft, but also knowing neither the Giants nor the Braves would be able to land him. They figured, and quite right, that the Pirates would have first crack and would grab him."

Clemente didn't have much of a chance at Montreal, where he batted only .257. He played only sparingly and spent most of his time as a pinch-hitter or a pinch-runner or played in the outfield in the late innings. Quite possibly, the Dodgers were trying to hide him.

The Dodgers' explanation is sound. "We knew we were going to lose him," Buzzy Bavasi once said, "so why spend time developing him for another team? We preferred to have him on another team to heckle the Giants."

So, he's making it tough for the Dodgers, as a member of the surprising Pirates. (Les Biederman)

The World Champion Dodgers dropped both games of their twin bill with the lowly, but vastly improved Pittsburgh Pirates. The Buccos won by the scores of 10-1 and 11-3, winning the first game behind Bob Friend, who would later in the season be the NL's starting All-Star pitcher. In the previous season, the Pirates won only eight games against the Dodgers, while dropping 14.

In the opener, Friend, the 1955 ERA leader hurled a six-hitter, giving up the lone run on a home run to Jackie Robinson. The Bucs hammered young Sandy Koufax, who only pitched two-thirds of an inning, allowing five hits and four runs.

In the nightcap, the Bucs chased Dodger starter, Billy Loes in the second inning behind a bases loaded single by Roberto

Clemente and a home run by pitcher Vern Law. Roy Campanella homered for the Dodgers.

Campy's homer put the Brooklyn catcher in a triple tie with Ted Kluszewski of the Redlegs and Yogi Berra of the Yankees with 212 career homers, the most for active players.

The Dodgers early season struggles continued as they lost seven of their next eight, before winning 6-0 vs. the Cubs at Wrigley Field behind a Don Newcombe three-hitter to even their record at eight wins-eight losses..

To achieve greatness, it often takes some time! Sandy Koufax did not get his tenth career major league win until his fourth season. In five of his first six seasons he had losing records. Dodger teammate Duke Snider once stated, "early in Sandy's career he could not even throw it into the batting cage." Koufax pitched 12 major league seasons for Brooklyn and Los Angeles from 1955-'66. In his first six seasons he had a 36-40 record and in his final six seasons he posted a 129-47 record. In a five year stretch from 1962-66 he won five consecutive NL ERA titles, winning both the Cy Young and NL MVP Awards in 1963, when he won 25 games, had a 1.88 ERA, with 11 shutouts and 308 strikeouts. The great Yankee, Yogi Berra commented "I can see how he won 25 games, what I can't see is how he lost five!"

Traumatic arthritis in his pitching elbow ended Sandy's career early due to the threat of permanent disability. He walked away from baseball after the '66 season at the age of only 31, which many would consider a baseball players prime. Five years later at age 36 in 1972 Sandy Koufax became the youngest player ever elected into the Baseball Hall of Fame. To achieve greatness, it often takes some time!

Incensed because Brooklyn pitchers Sal Maglie and Ken Lehman threw baseballs at the clock atop the Crosley Field scoreboard and stopped the mechanism, General Manager Gabe Paul of the Cincinnati Redlegs issued a statement.

"It is hard to understand what possessed the Brooklyn players, whom I understand to be Sal Maglie and Ken Lehman, to commit an act of vandalism by putting the clock atop the scoreboard out of commission. The officials of the Brooklyn club are being advised of this bit of senior delinquency."

Maglie laughed off the accusation, remarking; "I think some balls being fungoid to our pitchers hit the clock. Some of us did throw at the scoreboard and maybe our control was so bad we hit the clock. If I did hit and stop the clock, I wouldn't admit it."

Major League Baseball has always had its share of characters, and 1956 was no exception. Duke Snider the fine outfielder of the Brooklyn Dodgers was not one to waste time when telling of his dislikes in an early season article in Collier's magazine, a prominent American magazine at the time.

"The truth is that life in the major leagues is far from a picnic," he said. "I feel I'd be just as happy if I never played another baseball game again. I have my reasons and I can tell you pretty quick. There are youngsters who throw keys and marbles at my head when I'm backed up close to the stands in some parks. There are the older fans who bounce beer cans off my legs during dull moments in the games. There are sports writers who know just about as much baseball as my four year old daughter, but write articles about what is wrong with me every time I go a couple games without a hit." With his endorsement fees and his World Series share, Snider said his income was about $50,000. "You can put up with a lot for that kind of money," he added.

Snider's tales of hardship did not set well with fans, sports writers, baseball executives and even some players. "We read the story in advance and didn't like parts of it," said Buzzie Bavasi, Dodger vice-president. "Snider couldn't deny he said those things."

The 29 year old Snider commented "when I was a boy growing up in Los Angeles I used to dream about playing in a World Series. Last autumn when I was playing in my fourth

World Series I was still dreaming.....about being a farmer!" (Roscoe McGowen)

The article which was titled "I Play Baseball for Money, Not Fun," rocked the baseball world at a time when outspoken comments were not in vogue. "Right near the beginning of the article, I stated that 'I'm not complaining, just explaining,' and it seems that some have overlooked that," said the Duke. (Collier's Magazine)

Many experts felt that Sam Jones of the Cubs had the best stuff of any National League hurler. He led the Cubs to a 12-1 shellacking of the Redlegs in an early season contest that featured home runs from Ernie Banks and Monte Irvin, as the Cubbies had a six run first inning off Art Fowler. Jones stuck out nine and hurled a four hitter for his first win of the season. Rookie Frank Robinson scored the only Redlegs run as he doubled in the eighth inning and scored on Ed Bailey's pinch hit single.

On May 12, 1955, Jones known as "Sad Sam" and "Toothpick" to his NL counterparts had thrown the first no-hitter in MLB history by a black pitcher. Jones who led the NL in strikeouts in '55, '56 and '58 was known for being wild and had what many considered one of the best curveballs in baseball. He had lost 20 games the previous season for the lowly Cubs. Sam "Toothpick" Jones had a career 102-101 record while pitching mostly for second division clubs.

In the AL, Billy Pierce, the crafty White Sox lefty became the first pitcher in either league to reach win number three, as he defeated the Kansas City Athletics 9-7 in Comiskey Park on April 27. Pierce admitted this was not one of his better efforts, as he gave up 12 hits in the route going performance. Pierce allowed four homeruns, including two to Harry "Suitcase" Simpson. The victory moved the Chisox to within one game of the first place Yankees.

Pierce continued on with his outstanding work as he helped keep the Sox near the top of the AL standings with a

13-3 record at the All-Star break.

The New York Yankees recently made a plea for an American League rule for the 1956 season to require the mandatory use of batting helmets or suitable head protection by the batters.

Living dangerously was the apparent motto adopted by two of the AL teams. When all the ballots were in six of the eight AL teams were in favor of the rule, while two clubs abstained from casting a vote. League President Will Harridge decided then to let remain a matter for the individual teams to decide.

After Willie Jones, Philadelphia infielder, was beaned by the Dodgers' Don Newcombe during spring training, he said; "The big guy (Newcombe) deliberately threw at me, he does it all the time during the regular season."

There is no doubt that the fact Jones was wearing a helmet when hit by a Newcombe fast ball saved him from serious injury. You can be sure that Jones is ready to endorse the product to the players on the two American League clubs that don't seem to think protective helmets are important.

"Of course, it's up to each player to use his own head on the matter," said Jones. "But if he decides to do just that without a little protection, he had better have a thick skull." (Oscar Ruhl)

The Cleveland Indians concession department is crediting Coach Tony Cuccinello with an assist, as the tidbit known as 'pizza pie' is proving to be a hot item for fans at the concession stands. Cuccinello is an avid fan of 'pizza pie' and indulges quite often.

With so many home runs pitchers are complaining that the baseball is juiced, and some are referring it as a "rabbit ball." Former Washington Senators pitcher Walt Masterson, now attempting a comeback with the Detroit Tigers stated; "When I grip that ball, I can hear that rabbit's heart beat."

Casey Stengel's answer to Lou Boudreau's statement that

Mickey Mantle could hit .400 if he bunted more often: "Why should Mantle do Boudreau any favors by bunting?"

Kansas City teammates call Hector Lopez "Lopy" because of the way he lopes in pursuit of a fly ball in the outfield. "He will be a great centerfielder if he learns to use his great speed," predicts Lou Boudreau, the A's manager.

The spring rains continually played havoc with the early season schedule and no team felt it more than the Milwaukee Braves, who saw their record drop to 4-3 on April 30, as they dropped a 2-0 decision to the St. Louis Cardinals and pitcher Tom Poholsky. The Braves had several rainouts and had not played for four days.

Poholsky bested veteran Warren Spahn on this final play day of April, as both worked impressively into the ninth inning. Poholsky used pin point control to master the Braves, hurling a two-hitter, walking only one and striking out four.

Spahn was almost equally efficient, as he allowed only three hits and one base on balls while also fanning four batters. Spahn was a ground ball machine as he induced numerous Cardinals into ground ball outs, as Braves first baseman Joe Adcock had 13 putouts.

The Redbirds won it in the seventh inning as they had back to back singles from Ken Boyer, Rip Repulski and Wally Moon, along with a groundout to score their two runs.

The visiting Cardinals moved their record to 6-3 in front of 6,800 disappointed Braves fans in Milwaukee County Stadium.

"Television is proving a boon to the game rather than a detriment," National League President Warren Giles said during a brief stop while traveling through Ohio. He added, "There is more interest in baseball this season than ever before and television must receive a great deal of the credit."

When Chicago photographers asked Willie Mays to pose holding a bat before the game at Wrigley Field, the Giants outfielder replied grinning: "No, let's have this one with a glove. You always want a bat." Manager Bill Rigney, who overheard the conversation observed, "Willie isn't so proud of his bat right now. But he'll come out of it." The Say-Hey Kid had showed signs of shaking his slump in the game that followed by belting two triples. Willie had only hit .189 against the Cubs last year. His two triples helped the Giants defeat the Cubs 2-1 on this day.

Cleveland hurler Herb Score continues to pitch in tough luck. Score, who lost to the Chicago White Sox 1-0, April 19, although he yielded only three hits, lost another tough one, this time to the Detroit Tigers on April 29. The sophomore jinx worked overtime to hand the Indians' southpaw another 1-0 loss, on a walk off in the bottom of the tenth inning at Detroit.

Score again gave up only two hits over the regulation distance, but the third hit, a home run by Bill Tuttle with two outs in the bottom of the tenth inning, broke up the pitcher's duel with the Tigers Billy Hoeft.

Hoeft, although allowing nine hits, kept the Indians at bay, as he struck out five Cleveland batters, all in key situations. Score fanned thirteen and only issued four bases on balls.

"Glove-stuffing" is a recognized occupation by the United States Department of Labor. It seems there are many hundreds of workers who make a living out of putting the stuffing in baseball gloves, instead of knocking the stuffing out of someone. (Bob Addie)

When the Yankee hitters were in a mini-slump, a relatively new Yankee hurler was quickly given his pitching orders for the day. The Yankees scored one run in the first inning and Casey Stengel took Tom Sturdivant aside and said: "This is it, boy. There's your big lead. Go out and protect it."

Pee Wee Reese and Roy Campanella were sitting side-by-side in the dugout at Cincinnati, watching the Redlegs take batting practice. They spotted Ked Kluszewski, whose benching for overweight had created quite a stir.

"You look pretty good to me," shouted Reese.

Campanella stood up, turned profile, puffed out his ample belly, and patted it fondly. "The difference," yelled Campy to Big Klu, "is that I've been carrying this thing around for a lot of years. I'm used to it." (Dick Young)

Much was being made about the knockdown pitches of Dodgers Don Newcombe and others, resulting in a warning by the umpires. Manager Walt Alston wanted to protect his ace pitcher, so he came out to the mound to cool Newk down.

"When I came out to the mound, Alston said, "Newk was muttering about the Cubs pitchers throwing at everybody, including him." Newcombe had just been hit an inning earlier. "Newk told me that he was going to keep on throwing at everybody, including the Cubs' pitchers," said Alston. "The umpires warned that if he did there would be a 10 game suspension. So, just as Newk was about to take the mound for the seventh inning, I took him out of the game. He was not happy, but I did it to keep him from hitting someone and getting a ten game suspension."

Incensed at being lifted by Alston, Newcombe fired the ball at the ground and stalked off the mound. (Roscoe Mc-Gowan)

Dodger skipper Walt Alston is no cream puff. When he managed Montreal he had a hard-to-handle player who broke the club rules. Alston tongue lashed the player but to no effect. He fined him with no results. Finally, one night the skipper shooed the other players out of the clubhouse and locked the door. Alston had no further trouble with the player. Oh, yes, Montreal won the pennant that season. (Max Kase)

The rumor going around baseball is that the Philadelphia Phillies had the first crack at getting Junior Gilliam and Joe Black from the Baltimore Elites of the Negro League. The Phils could have had the pair for a total of $2,500, but turned thumbs down on the offer. (Dick Young)

Conflicting umpiring decisions has its humorous aspect. Grady Hatton, a Cardinal benchwarmer, was needling umpire Art Gore who was officiating at third base. Hatton was referring to the fact that the umpiring crew of Gore, Lee Ballantine, Bill Jackowski and Shag Crawford had worked many of the Redbirds early season games, Hatton sang out.

"When are we gonna get some good umpires to work our games?"

Hatton repeated the impertinent question to Jackowski, who gave him the thumb.

"Oh, no, you don't," the player insisted, "you can't put me out."

"Why not?" The umpire roared.

"Because," Hatton grinned, "Gore already chased me."

Jackowski took the crack good naturedly and smiled. (Bob Broeg)

The Minor Leagues
(Down on the Farm)

The organizational scheme of minor league baseball was much different than it is today. The Pacific Coast League was just a step below the major league teams and many felt the PCL was the third major league. The open classification PCL was very important to all of baseball, as they had an abundant number of players that had seen time in the major leagues and the PCL served as the top farm team for several MLB clubs. There were a similar number of minor league teams as we see today, but the classification was much different.

In addition to the PCL the classification of teams was Triple-A, Double-A, Class A, Class B, Class C, and Class D. As the system would be compared today, the Triple-A leagues, the Double-A, and possibly the Single-A leagues would be similar. The similarity ends however, with the Class B, Class C and Class D leagues. An assumption would be that the

Class D leagues of 1956 would be like the Rookie Leagues of today, but that is not necessarily the case. Numerous older players and local legend players in the smaller town Class D Leagues were abundant in number, in many instances to help with attendance. If a Class D League in a small town had a former major leaguer or a former local star on the roster, it would greatly enhance the number of fans attending their games.

A young Harmon Killebrew along with Earl Weaver, both destined to be in the Hall of Fame later in their careers were playing in the Class A South Atlantic League.

Eighteen year old Willie McCovey, another future Hall of Famer was playing for the Danville Leafs in the Class B Carolina League.

There were six Class C Leagues, the Arizona-Mexican League, California League, Central Mexican League, Evangeline League, Northern League and the Pioneer League.

The Class D Leagues were larger in numbers, as there were eight leagues, the Alabama-Florida League, Florida State League, Georgia State League, Georgia-Florida League, Midwest League, Nebraska State League, Pennsylvania-Ontario-New York League, known as the PONY League and the Sooner State League.

Some sort of order was necessary, as one could search the rosters of the Class C and Class D league teams and not find a single player that would ever grace a major league roster. The signing bonuses of the marginal or fringe prospects were basically non-existent, so clubs could stock the lower level leagues without a great deal of expense. Most of the small town teams in the lower classifications operated on a shoestring budget, but provided lots of summer entertainment for their townspeople.

During the '56 season the St. Louis Cardinals and Milwaukee Braves each had 15 minor league teams, Brooklyn had 14, while others had as many as 12. At the other end of the spectrum, both the Philadelphia Phillies and Baltimore Orioles had only eight minor league operations. The Boston Red Sox had seven teams, while the Chicago White Sox had only six. Each of these teams with a lower number of minor league support were attached to a PCL franchise, except the White Sox. The Pittsburgh club had no Triple-A team, but a strong affiliation with the Hollywood Stars of the PCL.

In addition, the Yankees, Cardinals and Dodgers each had a second Triple-A club, while the Cincinnati Redlegs Triple-A team, the Havana Sugar Kings of the International League provided nightly entertainment for visiting clubs that was not always safe and secure!

Frank Verdi, who years earlier had a "cup of coffee" with the New York Yankees, as a late inning defensive replacement for Phil Rizzutto, was hit with a bullet in Havana while coaching. Verdi was coaching third base for the Rochester Red Wings, the St. Louis Cardinals Triple-A team in an extra inning game with the Havana Sugar Kings. The Havana club was stocked with players by the Cincinnati Redlegs. The game was in extra innings when shots were heard throughout the stadium. Fortunately, Verdi was wearing a plastic liner in his helmet when a bullet struck him, deflected off his helmet and grazed his shoulder. Verdi was not seriously injured, but from time to time there were other incidents in the Sugar Kings Stadium.

The International League was appropriately named, as there were teams both north and south of the United States. The Brooklyn Dodgers Triple-A team was the Montreal Royals. The Toronto Maple Leafs who won the International League title was affiliated with several teams in their working agreement. At one time the International League had teams in San Juan, Puerto Rico and Ottawa, Canada.

Batting helmets were now required for batters, obviously for safety reasons. The Eastern League introduced a new helmet rule in an attempt to speed up play, as they adopted a rule requiring the batsman to continue to wear the protective helmet until returning to the dugout. In stressing the enforcement of this rule league president Thomas H. Richardson explained that "a base runner can be hit on the head just as easily as a batter."

In the Class B Southwestern League, manager Art Rowland of San Angelo charged that the Pampa team was using baseballs held over from last season. He protested a 7-6 loss to the Oilers saying they switched to the old balls in the third inning after they had taken a 5-0 lead. The Colts skipper charged in his protest that the baseballs were used by the Oilers when they were in the West Texas-New Mexico League last season, and that they are not official balls because they do not bear the signature of Southwestern President W. J. Green.

In the Class C Evangeline League, based in Louisiana, there were more serious problems. The Baton Rouge Rebels were forced to forfeit a game to the Lake Charles team because of a ban on playing against Negroes. They temporarily avoided the segregation problem for a series with Lafayette by shifting the two scheduled games to Lafayette.

The Baton Rouge Recreation and Parks Commission, which owned Goldsby Park, had announced before the season that Negroes would not be permitted to play there. Lake Charles and Lafayette were the only clubs in the league with Negro players.

The league made a temporary decision on the controversial segregation issue, with a statement that said Baton Rouge had three choices: (1) forfeit all home games, (2) play all such games on the road, or (3) drop out of the league.

Lake Charles, making its first visit of the season to Baton Rouge entered into "a gentleman's agreement" for the game scheduled on April 27. The Lake Charles manager benched his two Negro players, while in turn Baton Rouge played without their two regulars at the same positions.

However, for the second game of the series, Lake Charles

announced that the agreement would not continue, as they submitted their batting order with the two Negro regulars in the lineup. The Baton Rouge president of operations announced that the game had been "postponed" because of the recreation commission's segregation policy. However, the Evangeline League president, after receiving a report from the game's Umpire-in-Chief, awarded a forfeit victory to Lake Charles.

The Triple-A American Association had more than its share of future Major League players. Jim Bunning was pitching for Charleston, Ralph Terry and Tony Kubek were with Denver and Roger Maris was with Indianapolis.

In a sign of the times, one of the league's leading hitters, Carroll Hardy, who at the time was hitting a robust .362 was summoned on May 21 by the draft board for induction into military service. Hardy, who was an outstanding athlete, had also played pro football with the San Francisco 49ers. He asked for a deferment, but was denied due to public opinion.

After two weeks of action the Triple-A International League was full of names that would go on to have outstanding major league careers. No one was more noticeable than the great LeRoy "Satchel" Paige, who after his first four appearances sported a 1-0 record with an ERA of 0.00. Paige had joined the Miami Marlins at the start of the season with only four days of spring training. He chalked up a four hit shutout over the Montreal Royals in his first start. Before the game the fabulous "Satchmo" told reporters he was 49 years old, but then quickly added "maybe you had better add a couple to that." Paige who was listed at age 56 needed only 83 pitches for the seven inning shutout. It was the second game of a doubleheader and the 3-0 win was played in only one hour and thirty-eight minutes (1:38) before over 5,000 fans in Miami.

International League President Frank Shaughnessy ruled that Paige's "hesitation pitch" was legal. "If it was legal in the

American League, it's legal in our league," said Shaughnessy.

Paige had made his MLB debut with Cleveland on July 9, 1948 at age 42, when he was 6-1 with a 2.48 ERA for the Indians on the way to the World Series. He had last pitched for the St. Louis Browns in 1953. Some twelve years later, in the 1965 season he was the oldest MLB pitcher ever at age 59 when he pitched for the Kansas City A's. Paige's first pro season was in 1926 with Chattanooga in the Negro League. His last professional season came 40 years later. His MLB career marks are 28-31 with a 3.29 ERA while pitching for Cleveland, the St. Louis Browns and the Kansas City A's.

The Hall of Famer and two-time AL All-Star, Paige displayed a lot of wisdom in his legendary quotes, "How old would you be if you didn't know how old you are?" Perhaps his best was "age is a question of mind over matter. If you don't mind, it doesn't matter."

The Carolina League saw an umpire as well as a player get tossed! Umpire Bull Newsome and Al Barbee, Winston-Salem outfielder, were suspended indefinitely by the Carolina League, as a result of a rhubarb at Wilson, during which the umpire, with one punch, struck Twin Manager George Hausmann on the eye and Barbee on the shin. Barbee, in retaliation, hit the umpire with a bat.

In the seventh inning, after Newsome had cleared the Winston-Salem bench because of jockeying over several close decisions, Barbee stepped to the plate to take his at bat and exchanged words with the umpire, who was working behind the plate. While Barbee was still arguing, Newsome ordered the pitcher to throw and called two strikes on Barbee, the Twins outfielder.

Hausmann, who was coaching at third, rushed to the plate, stepped between Barbee and umpire Newsome and protested the called strikes. Newsome ordered Hausmann from the game and a heated argument followed. Barbee shoved Newsome and the umpire threw a punch which glanced off Hausmann's eye and struck Barbee, standing behind him, on the chin.

Barbee, still holding his bat, swung it and caught the umpire across the back. Hausmann grabbed Barbee from swinging the bat again. The umpire then ejected Barbee, too.

In baseball the box score is used to provide statistical representation about a specific game. It essentially summarizes the game and is informational in highlighting the individual performances of each player.

To have a basic knowledge of the game of baseball one should learn the value of understanding the box score. The abbreviations of offensive statistics, as well as pitching and defensive statistics tell the story of how each game was played. By learning how to read baseball statistics, fans can expand their appreciation and knowledge of the game. One can essentially recreate a game that was played many decades ago, with a great deal of accuracy.

The baseball box score has been improved through the years to give fans an even better understanding of how each particular game evolved.

Baseball's Golden Season

A Typical 1956 Baseball Box Score

Brooklyn Dodgers vs. St. Louis Cardinals
Thursday, May 3, 1956

Brooklyn	AB	H	O	A	St. Louis	AB	H	O	A
Gilliam, lf	5	2	3	0	Blasingame, ss-3b	5	1	2	3
Cimoli, lf...	0	0	1	0	Schoendienst, 2b	4	2	4	4
Reese, ss...	3	1	1	4	Musial, rf	4	1	0	0
Snider, cf...	4	1	6	0	Boyer, 3b	4	2	1	4
Campanella, c	3	2	4	0	cSchofield, ss	0	0	0	0
Hodges, 1b	4	1	8	2	Moon, 1b	4	3	9	0
Robinson, 3b	4	1	0	2	Virdon, cf	4	1	3	0
Furillo, r	4	2	1	0	Repulski, lf	4	2	4	0
Neal, 2b	4	1	1	2	Sarni, c	4	0	4	1
Newcombe,p	4	0	2	0	Flowers, p	0	0	0	0
Labine, p	0	0	0	0	Miller, p	0	0	0	0
					aHemus	1	0	0	0
					Jones, p	1	0	0	0
					bFrazier	1	0	0	0
					Jackson, p	0	0	0	1
					dCooper	1	0	0	0

```
Brooklyn..................................4 0 3   0 0 0   0 0 0 - 7
St. Louis................................. 1 0 0   0 0 0   2 0 0 - 3
```

Pitchers	IP	H	R	ER	BB	SO
Newcombe (Winner 3-1).........	8*	11	3	3	0	2
Labine.............................	1	0	0	0	0	1
Flowers (Loser 1-1)...............	2/3	2	4	4	1	1
Miller..............................	2 1/3	4	3	3	1	2
Jones..............................	4	2	0	0	2	1
Jackson.............................	2	1	0	0	0	1

*Pitched to 2 batters in ninth

aGrounded out for Miller in third. bFlied out for Jones in seventh. cRan for Boyer in eighth. dCalled out for Jackson in ninth. R-Reese, Snider, Campanella 2, Hodges, Robinson, Furillo, Blasingame, Moon, Repulski. E-Blasingame. RBI – Campanella 2, Furillo 2, Robinson 2, Hodges,Schoendienst, Repulski 2. 2B – Reese, Furillo, Blasingame, Musial, Moon, Schoendienst. 3B – Robinson. HR – Campanella, Robinson, Furillo, Repulski. SH – Reese. DP – Reese, Neal Hodges; Blasingame, Schoendienst & Moon. LOB – Brooklyn 8, St. Louis 7. Umps – Conlan, Donatelli, Englen, Delmore. T – 2:41. Attendance – 14, 734.

CHAPTER TWO

Spitballs, Bullpens and Batting Helmets
(Standings as of May 4, 1956)

American League				National League			
Team	**W**	**L**	**GB**	**Team**	**W**	**L**	**GB**
New York	9	5	---	Milwaukee	5	3	---
Chicago	5	3	1	St. Louis	7	5	---
Cleveland	8	5	½	Brooklyn	8	6	--
Washington	8	7	1 ½	Cincinnati	7	6	½
Boston	6	6	2	New York	7	6	½
Kansas City	5	7	3	Pittsburgh	7	7	1
Detroit	5	8	3 ½	Philadelphia	5	7	2 ½
Baltimore	5	10	4 ½	Chicago	3	9	4

With approximately three weeks of the season in the books, numerous games had been washed out. The Milwaukee Braves led the way with over a half dozen rain-outs, while many others were played in cold and dreary conditions. A horrendous stretch of early season bad weather probably cost the Braves alone over 200,000 paid admissions.

The Milwaukee club actually had nine rainouts in two weeks, and two of the early season postponements were on Sundays, including a doubleheader with the Brooklyn Dodgers.

The Milwaukee franchise which relocated to County Stadium from old Braves Field in Boston in 1953 had been a league leader in attendance, drawing over two million annually. Even with a tremendous amount of interest and a tight pennant race it would prove to be a difficult endeavor for the Braves to reach another two million in attendance after all the rainouts and bad weather. However, with an exciting baseball club that was just a year away from back to back World Series appearances (1957-58), the Braves did indeed draw over two million fans.

There was quite a difference in the number of teams in 1956 (16), as the number has just about doubled in franchises today (30). There was a growing list of declining stadiums in '56 compared to the large number of outstanding facilities currently today hosting MLB franchises. Times were different, affordability was different, the number of people in America was far less and there were a lot of factors that made attendance at Major League Baseball games oftentimes difficult for many.

In 1956, of the sixteen teams, eight of them drew over a million fans, with the Braves at two million averaging over 26,000 per contest. By comparison, in 2018, 29 of the 30 MLB teams drew over one million fans, with the dismantled franchise in Miami the only team to fall short of one million. The 2018 Los Angeles Dodgers were the top drawing team, with almost four million fans coming through their turnstiles. Seven additional teams drew three million and 12 more major league teams drew two million or more. The 2018 season by comparison, had a similar early season stretch of bad weather to that of the '56 season years ago.

The average number of fans to attend a 1956 Major League Baseball game was about 14,000, while in 2018 that number approached 28,000 per game. Both years had far more than the average number of early season rainouts.

Even in 1956, when the Opening Day for MLB was traditionally two or three weeks later than it is today, Tom Yawkey, the President of the Boston Red Sox and the "Dean" of club owners was outspoken regarding how baseball should handle early season weather. Yawkey submitted legislation attempting to bar major league teams from playing night games prior to May 1. "Baseball is a warm weather game," stated Yawkey. "I can't understand why fans, players and officials should be subjected to games under adverse weather conditions. It is difficult enough to play day games before May 1 when the weather is unsettled, let alone play at night." Yawkey reiterated that he was not trying to tell club owners how many night games they should play each season, saying "each owner knows what works best for his club and city." (Hy Hurwitz)

Rain and cold weather, or the combination of both resulted in eight of the 22 night games in 1956 scheduled in the month of April to be rained out.

Management was not alone in urging the barring of early season night contests. Many of the players were actually asking for a barring of night games before May 1.

Perhaps those in charge of the current Major League Baseball scheduling should take a look, even some 60 plus years later the same problems continue. Players nowadays come from the warmth of Florida and Arizona after completing spring training and delve immediately into cold weather games.

"There is new agitation against the double-header. In this day of the three-hour game, say those who would abolish them, the double-header is obsolete. The fans walk out on them, as they did recently when fewer than 2,000 of the original crowd of over 25,000 remained for the finish of White Sox-Cleveland marathon at Comiskey Park. The customers get enough baseball in one game." These are thoughts of

John Hoffman, sports writer of the Chicago Sun-Times early in the 1956 season.

Night baseball was on the upswing in 1956 as each year more and more games were being scheduled for night activity. There were a record number of 481 night games, 253 in the National and 228 in the American, scheduled for the '56 season. In the previous season (1955) there were 443 games played under the lights in the majors.

It had been 21 years since the introduction of night ball to the major leagues. On May 24, 1935 the Redlegs and Phillies played the first game under the lights, with Cincinnati winning by the score of 2-1. The second set of lights for night games was not put in place until June 15, 1938 when the Brooklyn Dodgers turned on the lights in Ebbets Field.

Scheduling has always and will continue to be controversial. Even today, with the benefit of computer scheduling there are unfair situations that cause problems for teams on the coasts to travel far more distances than those located in the central part of the country. Baseball franchises have always had a desire to open their season in mid-week due to the fact that season Opening Day contests are almost always sellouts, regardless of the day of the week. No matter the weather, Opening Day brings excitement, yet today, we see just two days later a northern located team playing a night game in early April or late March, resulting in a very small turnout of fans. It happens often, as television rules! What a great idea if MLB of today could take Mr. Yawkey's idea to heart and prohibit night baseball before the first of May?

Some things never change! Hecklers in major league ballparks were even more of a problem during the 1950's than they are today. Baseball players today and from yesteryear expect to be verbally abused. Players in the 1950's did not like it, and certainly players of today would not accept the physical abuse that players faced during the '50's.

Most 1956 bullpens were located down the right and left

field foul lines, yet many were uncovered, creating problems with weather, in particular the hot sun. The New York Giants played in the Polo Grounds, where the bull pens were far out in left field and in right-center field. The bull pens were actually in the playing area. This was possible because of the unique layout of the rectangular shaped Polo Grounds where the left center and right center corners were about 450 feet from home plate. Although any ball hit into the bull pen areas was in play, there was no record ever of any relief pitcher or catcher interfering with a hit ball or an outfielder in the Polo Grounds.

Although the high wall and canopies offered protection, the fans were still close enough to abuse bull pen players, both verbally and with projectiles. One plus about the Polo Grounds bull pens is that they were located near the center-field clubhouse, where a player could sneak in for a sandwich, or a cigarette.

The National League bullpens in St. Louis, Cincinnati and New York were unsheltered and drinking water was not even provided in New York, St. Louis and Chicago. In the eye of the players the ideal bullpen would be away from the crowd, out of the manager's sight and would be furnished with a snack bar, a smoking lounge and a bar!

Fabulous Forbes Field in Pittsburgh was also considered for hazardous duty pay, as longtime fans will remember that in spacious Forbes, the batting cage was always in play. Once batting practice ended, the grounds crew simply pulled the huge cage out into the depths of the outfield where it remained during the game.

In Connie Mack Stadium in Philadelphia the mound was so low and the bull pen warmup mounds so close together, that if two pitchers were warming up at the same time, they would often bump into each other.

Joe Gariagiola, a former player and broadcaster always said "the bull pen is supposed to be a place for warming up pitchers. That's what it is a little bit of the time, but mostly it's for eating peanuts, creating make believe games, trading insults with fans, hiding from the manager and second guessing him."

In the old Yankee Stadium the bull pens were located in the exits in left and right field. Vendors carrying beer, popcorn and peanuts as well as fans often walked through the runways. Harvey Kuenn, the Detroit Tigers player representative reported that in Cleveland's Municipal Stadium the bleacher fans continually threw vegetables, bottles, cans and old newspapers at the bull pen pitchers and catchers. Kuenn also said that Yankee Stadium as well as Comiskey Park was just as bad.

Records were strewn all over Wrigley Field, and relief pitchers performed like heroes, as the Giants defeated the Cubs, 6-5 in seventeen innings on May 2. The Giants used all 25 men for a major league record, and when the Cubs put 23 men in the lineup, the total of 48 was an all-time high for a game.

Eight pitchers for the Giants tied a National League record, and was one short of the American League mark. The Cubs Don Hoak equaled the major league record and set a new NL high by fanning six times in the game.

The game was the longest in innings played for the season and in time it was only six minutes short of the 5:19 record by Brooklyn and Boston in 20 innings in 1940.

The game was won when Alvin Dark doubled in the seventeenth with one out, advanced to third on a wild pitch and scored on Daryl Spencer's sacrifice fly.

In addition to Hoak's fantastic fate of fanning against six different pitchers, Monte Irvin came up five times and was retired by five different pitchers. But Whitey Lockman's journeying may have been the strangest record of all, Whitey started in left field, went to first then switched back to left, and finished at first. (Joe King)

After Baltimore newspapers mistakenly advertised young sensation Herb Score as the Cleveland starter for the May 3 game with the Orioles, 12,373 fans braved damp weather to show up at Memorial Stadium. Mike Garcia, who turned in a 7-1 Cleveland victory, kidded his young mound mate with: "If they had announced me, there would have been an even bigger crowd."

Frank Robinson, rookie outfielder of the Redlegs, narrowly missed hitting for the cycle against the Phillies, May 6. The twenty-year old youngster tripled in the first inning, homered in the third, doubled in the fourth and was deprived of a single in the sixth when Shortstop Granny Hamner made a dazzling stop of his hard smash.

May 6 was a big day for young players. Alvin Dark, the New York Giants' captain, spotted the tipoff in Vinegar Bend Mizell's delivery which enabled Willie Mays to steal four bases against the Cardinals' lefthander in the 5-4 New York win in St. Louis, in the second game of a double-header.

Mays stole second three times and third base once and his final theft of second in the ninth inning launched the winning two-run rally against a perplexed Mizell. The feat was rare, but not a record.

Mays said: "If I knew I was near a record, I could have taken third base easy." (The record was six) He added: "They didn't let me steal in the minors; I only began last year."

Both the Dodgers and Giants had aspirations of moving to better, more modern ballparks. Clubs were inspired by the tremendous increase in attendance by the Milwaukee Braves move from old Braves Field in Boston just three years earlier. Originally, both the Dodgers and Giants had plans to build new parks in the New York City area.

Dodger owner, Walter O'Malley said that in an undertaking as vast as the building of a new super-stadium, it was possible the Dodgers might have to move entirely out of Brooklyn. Having declared that the Dodgers will for certain be leaving

Brooklyn's Ebbets Field after 1957, O'Malley scheduled some of his home games in Jersey City, New Jersey. The Dodgers actually played seven National League contests in Roosevelt Stadium during the '56 season. It was an experiment to see how attendance would be in another venue, as Ebbets Field, built in 1913 was not aging gracefully and was in the middle of a deteriorating neighborhood.

O'Malley was trying to negotiate a newer, more fan friendly ballpark, but was not getting cooperation from the borough of Brooklyn. Make no mistake Mr. O'Malley was determined to move the Dodgers from Ebbets Field. Roosevelt Stadium was a multi-purpose stadium and was considered the best minor league park in America. There were flaws however, as in the Jersey City bull pens there were no mounds, just a slab set into the ground, which greatly irritated bullpen pitchers during their warmup activity. Attendance for the New Jersey scheduled games proved not to be much of an improvement over Ebbets Field.

Horace Stoneman, owner of the New York Giants had similar ideas, as the Polo Grounds were not the delightful palace that they were once considered, and attendance was suffering. Stoneham thought a move to the West Coast would revitalize the franchise, and history has proven that he was correct. The Giants attendance of 629,000 in '56 was last in the National League. New York City was less than two years away from losing two of its hallowed franchises to the booming West Coast.

Many writers and baseball personnel felt that it was indeed a certainty that the Giants would soon be leaving New York and the rapidly deteriorating Polo Grounds. There were many predictions as to where the Giants would relocate, including a sure bet that the Giants will move to Minneapolis-St. Paul, which has a new stadium erected and waiting for a major league franchise. Many believed the transfer would happen after the 1957 season. In truth, the actual relocation would ultimately be much farther to the west.

The following year (May of 1957) National League owners voted unanimously to allow both the New York Giants and Brooklyn Dodgers to move to San Francisco and Los Angeles, respectively. There were a few strings attached, one being that both teams had to move or neither could. The people of New York City were heartbroken, while the West Coast baseball fans were overjoyed. Baseball would be forever changed, as it now would be played from coast to coast

Two seasons later, in the 1958 season we would find the Los Angeles Dodgers playing in the Los Angeles Memorial Coliseum which was very difficult to configure for baseball. With a seating capacity of over 90,000 the Coliseum was the largest ballpark ever to host major league games.

Down the left field line it was only 250 feet, with a 40 foot screen atop the fence to cut down on the number of home runs. Pop flies were often home runs while there were 440 foot fly outs to right field. Left-handed batting Wally Moon joined the Dodgers in 1959 and learned to hit opposite field fly balls over the 250 foot screen, they were called "Moon Shots." The Dodgers played for four seasons in the Coliseum while Dodger Stadium was being built in Chavez Ravine, and quite often the stands were full, and the games had their own version of excitement. In game five of the 1959 World Series a record crowd of 92,706 watched the Dodgers lose 1-0 to the Chicago White Sox.

Horace Stoneman's transplanted Giants played in Seals Stadium for two seasons before moving to Candlestick Park. Seals Stadium had been a minor league park for decades and was a roofless, single-level-grandstand stadium. It was the smallest stadium in the major leagues and people loved watching games there, all the 22,900 seats were close to home plate. The Giants blasted the Dodgers, 8-0, in the first major league game played in San Francisco on April 15, 1958.

One of the early season highlights of the 1956 season

would have to be the Dodgers' Carl Erskine's no-hitter against the Giants on May 12 at Ebbets Field. It was the right handers second career no-no, as previously on June 19, 1952 he hurled a masterpiece against the Cubs.

In his latest no-hitter, Erskine struck out only three men while the Giants got only two men on base. Willie Mays walked with two out in the second inning and Alvin Dark walked to start the fourth.

It was in the fourth that Carl needed the two saving plays he got, Jackie Robinson's diving catch of Mays' low liner and Carl Furillo's over the shoulder catch of Daryl Spencer's long drive.

Here is Erskine's account of the ninth inning. "In the ninth I got one high and tight to Lockman and Whitey hit it out of the park, just foul. You know that grounder he hit back to me, I actually stopped that one with the back of my glove. When Dark hit the final ball back to me, I knew I had the no-hitter. I took my time with the throw and even then Gil Hodges was yelling at me not to hurry." (Roscoe McGowen)

Heretofore, the Cincinnati Reds had always been called the Redlegs, but as the season wore on many fans and sportswriters alike were beginning to call them "the Reds." The Redlegs finished the month of April strong and actually moved briefly past the Dodgers into second place on May 2 when they won their sixth straight contest, walloping five homers to outslug the Dodgers 10-6. Outfielder Gus Bell hit two homers, while George Crowe subbing for Ted Kluszewski at first base and Wally Post and Ray Jablonski each had one four bagger. Duke Snider, Roy Campanella and Sandy Amoros all homered for the Bums in the eighth inning.

A successful seventeen game home stand against all rivals except the Cardinals convinced many observers, including rival players that the Redlegs were going to have a lot to say about where the NL pennant will fly next year.

The Mutual Broadcasting System's Game of the Day radio programming covered the Yankees and the Giants three games each during the week of May 16 to 22. Yankee games with the Indians, White Sox and Tigers were aired, while the Giants were on the nationwide network for one game with the Braves and two with the Cardinals. What fans did not realize that the "Mutual Game of the Day," although serving the nation with their outstanding broadcasts, were very limited in the travels of the broadcast crew. Most of the games that were broadcast were from stadiums that were all in close proximity to one another, as it often proved difficult for the broadcast crew to travel from one city to another from day to day.

When Ernie Banks homered against Robin Roberts on May 4, the Cub shortstop continued his all-or-nothing record against the Phillies ace. The hit was only the fifth by Banks against Roberts, but all of them have been homers, four coming last season. The two run homer by Banks in the fourth inning enabled the Cubs to defeat the Phillies by the score of 2-1. The loss for Roberts was his first of the season after a 3-0 start.

When Pirates outfielder Frank Thomas blasted a home run in the sixth inning on May 6 at Wrigley Field, a disgruntled 12 year old Cub fan expressed his displeasure by tossing a candy apple that struck the surprised Pittsburgh outfielder in the mouth. Thomas was unhurt, but the youngster, who had been seated behind the Bucco dugout, was ushered from the park. Seems that Cub fans have not changed a great deal over the years, nowadays they voice their displeasure by throwing home run balls back onto the field from the bleachers.

Early Wynn, the Indians right hander, clocked at 40 miles an hour in a 30 mph zone while driving to Griffith Stadium, in early May, forfeited $15 collateral and continued on to the park where he took out his anger on the Senators with a 3-2 victory.

When the Indians returned home from a long mid-May

road trip, they found several of the new crash-type plastic helmets waiting for them. Al Rosen found one that fit and used it on the field and as well at bat. Bobby Avila attempted to do the same thing. He wore one for a couple days but suddenly had to discard it. He found that after getting a haircut, the helmet slipped down over his eyes. "I can't pad it," he complained, "and I can't find a smaller size. I just have to wait until my hair grows back."

When the Braves defeated the Pirates, 5-0 on May 8, it not only marked their fourth win in a row, but also it's fourth against as many different teams. Because of so many rainouts, the Braves played consecutive games against the Phillies, Giants, Dodgers and Pirates. It is doubtful that four games in four consecutive days against four different opponents had happened very often in MLB.

Mickey Mantle scored at least one run in ten consecutive games for the Yankees before drawing the collar in the Bronx Bombers' 3-2 win over the Orioles, May 11. The Commerce Comet failed totally in eight of the club's first 26 games.

When Phillies ace Robin Roberts earned win number five on May 24, defeating the Dodgers 6-4, he had almost half of the lowly Philadelphia club's win total. The Phils were at 12-22, in seventh place, just ahead of the Cubs. Roberts continued to give up the home run ball, as Duke Snider, Carl Furillo and Jackie Robinson all homered for the Dodgers. On pace to set a record for the most homers in a season, Roberts' pinpoint control made most of the homers single shots, as he seldom walked batters. Willie "Puddinhead" Jones blasted two homers for the Phillies, both off Don Drysdale.

Cardinal reliever Lindy McDaniel moved his record to 4-0, working in relief of starter Tom Poholsky, as the Redbirds moved to within one game of the Braves with a come from behind 11-9 win in St. Louis over the Cubs in the first game of a twin bill. In the nightcap, Stan Musial and Ken Boyer each homered to back the route going performance of lefty,

Wilmer "Vinegar Bend" Mizell, as the Cards won by the score of 12-2. Mizell hurled a five hitter and struck out 10 would be Cub hitters.

Also, on May 24, Mickey Mantle continued his onslaught of American League pitchers, leading the Yankees to an 11-4 victory over the Tigers in Detroit. Mantle, leading both leagues in hitting and slugging, belted his seventeenth homer of the year to go with four singles, boosting his batting average to .421. The Bronx Bombers had a five game lead over the second place White Sox.

How will Mickey Mantle counter the Boudreau shift? When Lou Boudreau, the shift-maker, fashioned his latest for Mantle, Casey Stengel said he wasn't concerned, because Lou could not very well put men in the upper decks in right and left field, when Mickey "hits them pretty good."

That goes way back when some of the managers in the American League were trying shifts on Babe Ruth, who would just punch the ball into the left side of the field and then stand on second base holding his belly, while laughing.

Shifts undoubtedly have a psychological value, provided the batters for whom they are designed are hard-headed, as, for instance, Ted Williams was in the 1946 World Series, when the Cardinals fanned to their left whenever he went to bat. With the entire left side of the field wide open, he only rolled a bunt past third base one time. Meanwhile, he was lining out deep to the right fielder or being thrown out by the second baseman who was playing in short right field. Less stubbornness and more adroitness at the plate on his part very easily might have won the Series for the Red Sox. Ted was determined to beat the Cardinals 'his way.' In other words, they couldn't do that to him.

"If Mantle is sufficiently imaginative, which sometimes appears dubious, he can have a lot of fun with Boudreau or any other manager who tries to trap him in a shift. It's all right for Lou to say that he doesn't care how many singles Mickey gets if he does not hit the long ball, but an ambidextrous hitter with all that good speed could 'single' Boudreau to distraction, and cost him some ball games, too." (Frank Graham, New York Journal-American)

In Kansas City, A's lefty Tommy LaSorda had the longest outing of his career, as he went eight and two-thirds innings. Lasorda allowed only three hits, but his effort was hardly a masterpiece as he walked 10 White Sox batters. After Lasorda was relieved, the Sox rallied for two ninth inning runs to tie the score at 4-4. Sox manager, Marty Marion called on his ace, Billy Pierce to pitch the bottom of the ninth, who promptly walked Hector Lopez before giving up a long home run to Enos Slaughter for the 6-4 walk-off win for the A's.

A two-dollar bill, frequently regarded as jinx currency, was a good luck charm to Whitey Ford on May 28. When the Yankee southpaw stooped to pick up the rosin bag at the start of the second inning at Yankee Stadium, he found a deuce which had apparently blown out of the stands. Ford pocketed the money and went on to blank the Red Sox 2-0 to move his league leading record to 7-1.

Outfielder Irv Noren of the Yankees was the victim of a telephone hoax when the Bombers were in Detroit, May 23. Noren received a telephone call in his hotel room, in which the other party identifying himself as Hal Middlesworth of the Detroit Free Press, asked for his opinion of "the deal" sending Noren and Gil McDougal to the Tigers for Ned Garver and Ray Boone. Noren had several uneasy minutes before he was able to locate Manager Casey Stengel and learn that there had been no such deal.

The esteem in which Dale Long is held by his teammates was illustrated after the night game at Connie Mack Stadium on May 25, which the Pirates won as Long racked up his sixth home run in his record-breaking splurge and two singles for a three RBI performance.

The bus taking the Buccos back to the Warwick Hotel was

ready to depart when somebody noticed the absence of Long who was talking with reporters.

Nelson King, who was the winning pitcher, thanks to Long, rushed out and lay down in front of the bus. "This bus doesn't move until Dale Long gets on," King yelled. "He's our meal ticket!"

On May 28, Dale Long received the first curtain call ever in Forbes Field after he hit his eighth home run in his eighth consecutive game, when the Pirates defeated the Dodgers 3-2. The 32,221 fans in attendance, gave Dale a standing ovation as he circled the bases. They continued to applaud until he stepped out of the dugout to tip his cap. Long's streak was snapped the next day when Don Newcombe of the Dodgers shut out the Bucs. Dale Long had set a major league record that even Babe Ruth had not equaled.

Ironic that Dale Long, whose home run bombardment has been the sensation of the early season, was born on February 6, the natal date for Babe Ruth, the king of all clouters. Incidentally, two years ago (1954) Long reported to the Pittsburgh training camp at Fort Pierce, Florida, with very little money in his wallet. One night, after a game, he helped the team equipment custodian load trunks and received $5 for his efforts.

"I really needed that fin, too," said Dale, who has already earned approximately $3,500 for endorsements and TV appearances as the result of his homer binge. In the off-season Long officiates high school and prep football games in North Adams, Massachusetts, where he makes his home, and also works in the personnel department of an electric company.

The big reason why most baseball people say that Ted Williams won't retire after this season, according to second-guessers, is that he is about to sell his life story to the movies and the sale price would be affected by his decision to quit.

Jimmy Piersall, one of the top outfielders in the American League, marvels at teammate Mickey Vernon's batting technique. Vernon was hitting .357 at Memorial Day and was third among all AL batters. "He stands up there," Piersall describes Vernon, "like the most relaxed guy in America. He just swings his bat like it was a toothpick and he 'sings' while doing it. I sing, too, when I go up to hit, but obviously I don't know the right tunes."

Piersall is never one to mince his words. While watching the Washington Senators Eddie Yost break in a new glove, Piersall moved closer to watch him. "Where did you get that thing?" Piersall asked innocently, "At the corner drug store with a load of coupons?"

Quote from Baltimore pitcher Bill Wight: "There are two kinds of people who don't worry, those who are so smart they don't have to worry; and those who are too dumb to worry. It's my misfortune to be in neither group." (Oscar Ruhl)

The largest Memorial Day attendance since 1950 was recorded this year when 240,354 fans turned out for a full slate of double-headers in both leagues. For a similar schedule in '50, the crowd was 274,326. The majors' largest gathering was at Philadelphia, where over 35,000 saw the Dodgers split with the Phillies. The AL's largest crowd was at Baltimore, where just over 33,000 saw the Orioles sweep the Red Sox.

Vic Wertz, who has been suffering from dizzy spells, underwent an examination in Washington, and was assured that his trouble was not related to his attack of polio suffered a year ago. The Cleveland first baseman, admitting he was "plenty worried," added "I didn't know what to think when I started to get dizzy spells. I thought it might be something similar all over again." The medical staff told Wertz he was only suffering from a kidney infection.

Casey Stengel, who recently celebrated his sixty-fifth birthday, has no immediate intentions of leaving the Yankees for his comfortable home in Glendale, California. "I figure I'm going to be around here for maybe two more years," Stengel is reported to have confided to close associates.

Stengel is now serving the last of a two-year contract, with a salary reported to be $80,000 a year.

Talk of moving next year's (1957) World Series and the All-Star Game from daytime to night-time for television viewing ratings was apparently "just talk." Many observers believe that eventually both the World Series and All-Star Game will be seen by many more fans if the contests were played at night, or at least twilight, when millions of working people would be home from their jobs.

"It would seem that more people would be involved, but it just doesn't work out that way," said Tom Gallery, Sports Chief of NBC. "Our TV surveys and others that have been taken reveal that the ratings for these two events are right at the top, up with such spectacles as Mary Martin in Peter Pan, and you just don't get them any higher than that."

"Practically everything comes to a halt when the games are on anyway. Taverns and restaurants are packed," continued Gallery. "Thousands of workers see, or at least hear, the games in factories, offices and on the street. Just like they say in England, 'Everything stops for tea.' Well here, everything stops for the World Series!"

Gallery said if other groups were interested in making a change, he could see no objection to night-time or twilight staging of the baseball classics. "There are very few people in this country who miss the World Series, if they are interested in it. They get it one way or another."

There are approximately 80,000 fans per day in New York City who are interested enough to spend a dime by calling up the telephone company to get the World Series score. Presumably, they would represent a hard core of many thousands more who would watch by television or listen by radio if the games were played at night when they were home from their jobs.

What is most interesting is that during the 1955 World Series over a million people called their special correct time number to find out not only what moment of the day it was, but also whether the Dodgers or Yankees were ahead. The daily average of correct time calls is 73,750. That means during the World Series of last year the calls more than doubled. There were more than 79,938 more calls per day than during a normal period. (Carl Lundquist)

From this writers' longtime viewpoint, twilight starts might be good. But, the late starts dictated by television nowadays (2019) has late night endings of weekday World Series games often extending well into the wee hours of the morning, when people are sleeping in front of their televisions, instead of watching the game, or they have tuned out and gone to bed, because they have a work day the next day. Twilight or late afternoon games would benefit all of the United States time zones. The Eastern zone could watch the games after dinner, while fans in the Western time zone could enjoy a late afternoon contest.

Major League Baseball often talks about the many ideas as to how they can create more interest in the game, essentially to keep it moving. Whether it's implementing the pitch clock, number of mound visits, keeping the batters in the box, or whatever. I maintain that the only problem our great game has today is that the weekday World Series games need to be played at an earlier starting time! Television ratings would work themselves out. The youth of today who have followed their favorite teams and the long baseball season are deprived of watching this great sports spectacle, simply due to the lateness of the games. Twilight starts would give everyone an opportunity to see the climatic ending of the season!

After a lengthy time as general manager of the Chicago White Sox, Frank Lane, otherwise known as "Trader" Lane assumed the general manager duties of the St. Louis Cardinals just prior to the '56 season. Baseball has seen some strange individuals in their long history, and "Trader" Lane will rank with the best of them! He was one of the more colorful personalities in baseball all during his career which covered several decades and five major league teams.

Lane was hired after the 1955 season by Cardinal owner August Busch from the White Sox to resurrect the sagging fortunes of the Cardinals. Lane essentially had a blank check to do whatever it took to bring a pennant back to this once proud franchise. The Redbirds had finished in seventh place in '55 with a 68-86 record, and Busch was determined to again become a contender

In the first 17 days of May, Frank Lane made six deals involving 17 players and almost completely revised the Cardinal team. He traded for home run hitting Hank Sauer, obtaining him from the Cubs. He traded away stellar left-handed pitcher Luis Arroyo to the Pirates for righty Max Surkont. Then, on May 11 he engineered a blockbuster, trading pitchers Ben Flowers, Harvey Haddix and Stu Miller to the Phillies for Murry Dickson and Herm Wehmeier. Haddix had earlier authored a 20 win season.

"In parting with Haddix, Miller and Flowers, we traded away quantity for quality," said Frantic Frank. "We have the power with such fellows as Stan Musial, Ken Boyer, Wally Moon and Red Schoendienst. We have plenty of speed and good defense, but if you have everything else and don't have good pitching you can't win." Lane continued, "In the final analysis, it is pitching that will determine our pennant chances. Surkont, Dickson and Wehmeier are all experienced pitchers and will help us form one of baseball's best pitching staffs."

Just three days later on May 14, he traded Solly Hemus to the Phils for Bobby Morgan. He then followed up on May 16 with a trade that sent Joe Frazier and Alex Grammas to the Redlegs for Chuck Harmon. The next day he traded fan favorite, Bill Virdon to the Pirates for Bobby Del Greco and Dick Littlefield, in what history has shown was the worst deal Lane made in his tenure in St. Louis. Virdon, who had been the Rookie of the Year the previous season, hit .334 for the

Pirates and played 10 more good years.

Bing Devine who worked under Lane in St. Louis thought Lane was "addicted to trading. Some of his trades were nuts, and some were good."

Just a month later, on June 14 he traded Jackie Brandt, Littlefield, catcher Bill Sarni and Red Schoendienst to the Giants for Al Dark, Ray Katt, Don Liddle and Whitey Lockman. In trading away youth for experienced players, "Trader" Lane explained "I'll sign Methuselah if he can win for us."

Years later, Red Schoendienst would become the Cardinals manager and lead them to the World Championship on his way to the Hall of Fame. When Lane traded Schoendienst, who was one of the most popular Cardinals ever, it turned into a nightmare as Red Schoendienst helped Milwaukee beat out the Cardinals for the '57 pennant He even tried to trade Stan Musial to the Phillies for Robin Roberts, before owner, August Busch stopped him. He could not trade Musial, so he traded Stan's friend and roommate, Schoendienst.

Frank Lane stated early in the season that six Cardinals were untouchable,three of them were gone before mid-season! The final straw came when he removed the "Birds on the Bat" logo from the front of the jersey. The "Birds on the Bat" were absent for only one season, the only season in the Cardinals long history. Owner, Busch ordered that the "Birds on the Bat" must be returned to the uniform for the following season.

There was moderate success in bird land as the Cardinals would finish the '56 season in fourth place with a 76-78 record. The '57 season would bring excitement to St. Louis as the Cardinals flourished with an 87-57 record, but lost out to the Braves and Red Schoendienst. "Gussie" Busch had enough and when Frank Lane looked elsewhere for employment, Busch did not stop him. Many believe that Lane's penchant for bringing in older players caught up with the franchise. It was eight years later, in 1964 before the Cardinals again won the NL pennant and the World Series.

Lane continued trading all during his initial season, as 14 deals resulted in 35 players either coming to St. Louis or leaving. During his career as a MLB general manager, Frank Lane traded 690 players involved in 414 deals. He once traded a home run champion for a batting champion.

While most of the Major League Baseball games in 1956 were on average about 30 minutes shorter in time than today, there was constant chatter to keep the '56 games moving with more action. In a Sporting News article by Joe King whose weekly column was entitled "Clouting 'Em," King commented on the following proposal regarding the intentional walk.

Here was the proposal idea: James T. Gallagher, Rules Committee chairman, is willing to submit an intentional walk idea to his group, not so much as to push its adoption, as to get a consensus on the deliberate pass. "Suppose runners were allowed to advance one base every time a batsman was given four straight intentional balls? As it is, the manager averts a headache by waving a Musial or Williams to first base with a runner on second, in a pinch. Then he hopes for a double play by a lesser hitter. Under the proposal, the man on second would move to third. That would alter strategy and likely offer the big hitters more shots to break up a game. If no one was on base, the batter receiving the intentional pass would be automatically advanced to second." ((Joe King)

It certainly is worth noting that many of the thoughts and ideas of today to "keep the game moving" were prevalent back in 1956.

Beans Reardon, the legendary MLB umpire, on a recent visit to New York, recalled how Ford Frick, when he headed the National League, called him on the carpet for cussin' at ball players.

"They cuss me out, why shouldn't I cuss 'em back?" Beans offered in defense. 'Put them out of the game,' Ford counseled. 'Then I'd have to sit up all night making out reports,' the umpire protested. 'It's so much easier just to cuss 'em right back.'"

Baltimore pitcher Bill Wight, who is quite a talented cartoonist, is going to do some sketching for the Baltimore club but not of Paul Richards. "I learned my lesson when I was with Cleveland," chuckled Bill. "I drew one of Hank Greenberg (Cleveland General Manager) and before I knew it, I was traded." (Oscar Ruhl)

It was disclosed that the Detroit Tigers were one of the two American League teams which had declined to vote on the resolution offered by the Yankees to force all batters to wear helmets. Spike Briggs owner of the Tigers stated that it should be left up to the individual player if he wants to wear a helmet or not. "There is another angle," Briggs says, "if the AL was to force a player to wear a helmet, and he was injured seriously despite that, he would have the basis of a suit against his club and the league."

The Minor Leagues
(Down on the Farm)

In the Pacific Coast League, Ralph Kiner, who was serving as the San Diego general manager was asked if there was any thoughts of climbing back into uniform to give the Padres a lift at bat, the GM replied: "That is out. I've had it. I can still remember the aches and pains I had in my last days as an active player at Cleveland and how tough it was getting out of bed every morning."

Negroes were admitted to the grandstand at the Carolina League's Grainger Stadium in Kinston for the first time ever, May 9, but only about 35 took advantage of the new ruling which permits them to sit in a section adjacent to the bleachers. They were far outnumbered by Negro fans in the bleachers.

PCL President Leslie O'Connor denies he is trying to put a gag on managers and players. "The managers and players can talk to umpires as much as they ever did," O'Connor declared while attending a meeting of the local baseball writers' chapter in Los Angeles. "Only they must do it in a decent manner. I don't think the fans like to see the umpires cursed and reviled."

Concerning his speed-up plan, O'Connor said he wasn't trying to cut down on the time of games "but to speed up the action. A game can't last too long if it's full of action. We are not going to tolerate long arguments."

It is hard to believe, but time was allowed for arguing balls and strikes during the 1950's. The PCL set a 30-second limit on the time a batter may argue over a called strike and a one-minute limit for a player to resume action following an argument over other matters.

Baseball executives, managers, coaches and players all marvel at the accomplishments of Steve Bilko of the Los Angeles Angels of the PCL. At the Memorial Day mark, each team had played almost 50 games and Bilko was hitting .417, some twenty points higher than second place Dick Sisler of San Diego. In addition, Bilko had blasted 23 homers, more than double that of any other PCL player, and had 53 RBI's, more than any other two PCL hitters combined total.

In the American Association, the Denver Bears of the parent Yankees were making a shambles of the AA pennant race, leading by seven games on Memorial Day. Tony Kubek hitting at .342 was among the league batting leaders, while five Denver pitchers were ranked in the league's top ten in wins, led by soon to be Yankee, Ralph Terry with a 5-0 record.

In the Class B Carolina League, Willie McCovey, the eighteen year old Danville first baseman in just his second year of organized ball, batted in seven runs against High Point-Thomasville on May 27. McCovey had a homer, triple and double while sparking the Leafs to a 16-3 triumph over the Hi-Toms. His homer with two on highlighted a six-run rally in the opening frame.

Ray Mantle, brother of Mickey Mantle of the Yankees, broke loose with seven hits in 19 trips to the plate for a .368 pace in five games between May 23 and 27 after rejoining the Monroe Sports of the Class C Evangeline League.

Elwin (Preacher) Roe, the ex-Brooklyn mound ace who now runs a super market in West Plains, Missouri, was interviewed recently on television concerning major league hurlers who might be using the spitball.

"There are 12 or 14 pitchers I think use the spitball," drawled the Preacher. "I can't say for sure they're using it, but I taught about a dozen of 'em how," he explained.

Roe received nation-wide notoriety last year over an article in a national weekly in which he named the "spitter" as his money pitch in the closing stages of his major league career.

Montreal's George "Sparky" Anderson who stands just five-nine and weighs a mere 160 has been a real find for the Montreal Royals. The second sacker has led many fans to forget Charley Neal who excelled for the Royals last season before his promotion to Brooklyn. When the club opened a two week road trip in Rochester, Anderson was hitting a mere .467. In May alone he was hitting .518, prompting comments from many of the games legends.

Branch Rickey had once said of Eddie Stanky, "he can't hit, he can't run, he can't throw, but he is the most valuable player on his team." Frank Shaughnessy, the International League president said, "Sparky Anderson is a Stanky with ability."

Working his way up the chain, Anderson has made the All-Star team in every league he has played, 1953 in the California League, in '54 in the Western League and last season with Fort Worth in the Texas League. In the last off-season Sparky worked for Sears-Roebuck in Los Angeles, but wants to play winter baseball after the current season is over.

Three years later at the age of 25, Sparky spent the entire 1959 season with the Philadelphia Phillies, but hit just .218. This was his only season of playing Major League Baseball, but he went on to the Baseball Hall of Fame as he managed major league clubs for 26 seasons. Sparky Anderson won two World Series titles, in 1975 and '76 with the Cincinnati Reds and in '84 with the Detroit Tigers. He had over 2000 MLB wins.

Scheduling problems have persisted in the Class C Arizona-Mexico league, as president Tim Cusick announced he had awarded a forfeit to the Douglas team because of the Tijuana Colt's failure to show up for a game on May 16, but would not change the standings until he had ruled on two other games that the Colts missed at Cananea.

A misspelled word in a note of apology from Amarillo, sent to all other Western League teams, turned out to be perhaps more appropriate than first thought. General manager, Buck Fausett explained there is no dressing room for visiting teams in the present Amarillo park and that, until the new park is ready, the guests will have to change and shower at their hotel. Here's how Faucett's final sentence came out: "We know the lack of a dressing room is inconvenient, but we hope you will be patient and BARE with us." (Bill Bryson)

CHAPTER THREE

Yankees Surge to the Top
(Standings as of June 1, 1956)

American League				National League			
Team	**W**	**L**	**GB**	**Team**	**W**	**L**	**GB**
New York	29	13	---	Milwaukee	19	10	---
Chicago	18	15	6 ½	St. Louis	23	16	1
Cleveland	20	17	6 ½	Pittsburgh	21	15	1½
Boston	20	19	7 ½	Cincinnati	21	16	2
Baltimore	19	21	9	Brooklyn	19	16	3
Detroit	18	21	9 ½	New York	15	21	7 ½
Washington	16	25	12 ½	Philadelphia	12	22	9 ½
Kansas City	15	24	12 ½	Chicago	10	24	11 ½

In the National League early in the month of June, the Dodgers were at .500 with a 19-19 record. Pitchers Sal Maglie, Roger Craig, Carl Erskine and Don Newcombe all had their ups and downs in the early going and the rookie, Don Drysdale was inconsistent. Reliever Clem Labine pitched well for the Bums and kept them near the top of the standings with Milwaukee and Cincinnati.

Only Duke Snider hit well in the early portion of the season. Roy Campanella, Gil Hodges, Carl Furillo and Jackie Robinson, all stalwarts of the Dodgers hitting attack struggled to find their stride. Several wallowed in the .230 range before they would find their stroke later in the season.

Mickey Mantle's much discussed May 30 home run, which just missed being the first ball hit out of Yankee Stadium when it struck high up on the right field façade, actually doesn't rank with some of his other homers in the distance department.

The Reeves Analog Computer, an intricate computing machine, found that had the ball traveled an uninterrupted flight, its total distance from the bat to the point where it first hit the ground would have reached 481 feet.

The Yankee centerfielder previously hit a ball in Griffith Stadium, in Washington, that measured over 500 feet.

Enthusiasm of the fans in and around Pittsburgh for the Pirates continues sky-high. Employees of a Pennsylvania newspaper have printed their own souvenir World Series tickets and already have the Pirates playing the Yankees in the classic, scheduled to open in Forbes Field, on October 6. On the face of the ticket is printed: "The Milwaukee Braves will be in charge of the refreshment stand."

When Rocky Colavito and Vic Wertz homered off Don Larsen, June 9, it raised to 11 the number of round-trippers yielded this season by the Yankees right-hander, who gave up only eight during the entire 1955 season.

Pirate hurler Bob Friend extended his string of scoreless pitching against the Cardinals to 20 innings, June 8, when he defeated the Redbirds 3-0 in eleven innings. The Bucs right-hander also had blanked the Cards, 6-0, May 23.

On June 7, the Pirates lost to the Cubs 5-2, thus dropping out of the league lead, falling behind the Reds and Cardinals. The Pirates had held first place alone for three days, a spot that they have been unaccustomed to in recent years. Bob Rush, of the Cubs hurled a complete game six hitter for his fifth win of the season.

The Reds, who had finished in the second division for eleven straight seasons, pounded their way into first place by defeating the Phillies 8-5. Reds catcher, Smokey Burgess went 2 for 3 with a home run, while Wally Post had a three hit day. Working in relief, Joe Nuxhall got the win, with only one inning of work.

When the Reds climbed into first place on June 7, it marked the first time in 16 seasons that the club had held the top spot so late in the season. In 1940, as the Reds were on their way to the NL pennant, they were one game in front on June 7.

In the American League, Sherm Lollar, of the White Sox tied a major league record, June 8 when he was hit by a pitched ball three times as the Sox lost 5-3 to the Red Sox. The Chicago catcher was plunked each time by Willard Nixon. The last batter to be hit by a pitch three times in one game was Mel Ott, back in 1938.

After 53 games, Mickey Mantle was well on the way to the season that was predicted for him. In only 201 AB's, the Mick had 21 home runs to go with 53 RBI's, while hitting at a .388 clip.

Billy Pierce moved two months ahead of his victory pace of last season, when he hurled the White Sox to a 3-2 decision over the Boston Red Sox for his eighth triumph of the season. Last year, the lefty did not get his eighth win until August.

Another home run record fell before the bat of Dale Long, the Pirate slugger on June 9. With his seventeenth homer of the season off Vinegar Bend Mizell, Long completed the cycle of hitting a home run in every National League park this season. It was the earliest date in the history of the majors that a player had belted a four-bagger in each park of his league.

Long broke a record held by Eddie Matthews of the Braves, who had completed the park cycle on June 13, 1953 in Milwaukee's first season in the that city.

Brooklyn's Don Newcombe was one of their few bright spots in the early part of the season, as the World Champs struggled to stay above the .500 mark. Newk picked up his ninth win of the season on June 11, pitching the Dodgers to a 8-6 win in St. Louis. A couple of key errors made a loser out of Cards hurler Tom Poholsky who pitched well. Duke Snider continued on a tear as he blasted two home runs, while Wally Moon and Hank Sauer both homered for the Redbirds.

After two consecutive whippings by the Indians, by the scores of 9-0 and 15-8 in the first two games of the series in New York, the Yankees picked up a 6-0 win behind the superb pitching of Johnny Kucks. Becoming the right-handed ace of the staff, Kucks posted his seventh victory against three defeats, to equal the win total of teammate Whitey Ford. In the process, the Bronx Bombers defeated Bob Lemon, who was seeking his eighth win of the campaign. Billy Martin had three of the twelve Yankee hits, including a home run, as 47,465 fans witnessed the Yankee win.

Prior to the game, Yankee manager Casey Stengel sounded off! Despite the Yankees' position at the top of the American League race, Stengel threatened a wholesale shakeup to awaken the Bombers from their rut.

The Old Professor, upset at "the lousy baseball we've been playing," said, "Yeah, yeah, I know we're three games ahead, but we won't be long playing the kind of ball we are."

"Something's gotta be done," he continued, "the pitching has been horrible, we're not very good in the outfield and the infield has been far from perfect." Casey was particularly puzzled by his pitching staff, "not counting Whitey Ford, the only pitchers who have shown any improvement over last year are Johnny Kucks and Tom Sturdivant. I don't know what in the world is wrong with the other guys."

After three White Sox batters had been struck by pitches in a Yankee game, Casey Stengel denied he had given orders for his hurlers to throw at the batters. "My pitchers," said Casey, "have enough trouble following orders to throw the ball over the plate."

Chicago's Comiskey Park is one of the few stadiums in the majors which does not play the National Anthem before a game. Baltimore started out the same way until an indignant patriot reminded the Orioles that Baltimore was the birthplace of the National Anthem, written by a Baltimorean, Francis Scott Key, at Famed Fort McHenry during the War of 1812. The O's haven't missed since.

The White Sox consistently have led the league this year in hit batsmen. Instead of being the "Hitless Wonders," as they are often referred to, they may wind up as the "Get-Hit Wonders." Every club has its "get-hit" experts. Chicago's expert is Minnie Minoso while Washington's is Eddie Yost.

The Cincinnati Reds, known as some of baseball's best sluggers were recently discussing the merits of NL pitchers during a pre-game dugout chat. It was largely agreed that the Dodger's young pitcher, Sandy Koufax throws harder than the Cardinals Vinegar Bend Mizell.

Working for GM Frank Lane may be an aggravation, but it's never dull. Manager Fred Hutchinson of the Cardinals often disagrees with his impatient boss. One case in point involved Stu Miller, the soft throwing hurler. Hutch wanted to get rid of him; Lane thought Stu was worth keeping, and told Hutch to pitch him. "Okay," said the Cardinal Manager, "I'll pitch him, which game do you want to lose?" Shortly thereafter, Miller was traded.

Virtually overnight, the great hatred between Sal Maglie and Carl Furillo, which was ongoing when on opposite teams, has developed into a warm friendship. On the road, Sal rooms alone. After a night game, he'd send out for a batch of barbequed ribs and invite Furillo up to his room to devour them.

Another prodigious homer by Mickey Mantle, who smashed a ball that hit on top of the right field stands in Detroit and then bounced out onto Trumbull Avenue, powered the Yankees to a 7-4 victory over the Tigers. "The Mick," batting left-handed against Paul Foytack, belted the drive with two men on base and two out in the eighth inning. Since the park had been remodeled in 1937, only Ted Williams had ever hit a fair ball out of Briggs Stadium. Don Larsen working in relief of Bob Turley picked up the win, his fourth of the season against one loss. Larsen pitched six plus innings and only allowed three hits.

Mantle, who has been warned repeatedly by Casey Stengel for swinging at bad pitches, actually hit a pitch out of the strike zone when he drove the June 18 record breaker out of Briggs Stadium. According to Frank House, the Tigers catcher, it was "a fast ball a little inside and up around the shoulders. It wasn't a fit pitch to hit." Before Mantle's blast, House said, "Mickey, you ain't gonna hit one out of here today, that wind coming in from right field is just too much for you."

Just two days later, the groundskeepers at Briggs Stadium turned on the sprinkling systems to protect Mantle from enthusiastic fans after Mickey hit two more home runs. The Yankee star was greeted by a couple of young boys upon returning to center field after he powered his second home run of the night in the eighth inning. When he took his position in the ninth inning a large group of fans, mostly boys, clustered around the slugger. At the conclusion of the game, before many of the 47,756 spectators could leave their seats, the underground sprinkling system was turned on and Mickey jogged to the clubhouse without any interference.

Mantle, the slugging Yankee outfielder who is making a strong bid to break Babe Ruth's home run record of 60 for one season, was 18 days and 18 games ahead of the Babe's mark for a comparable period through June 20.

With the aforementioned two circuit blasts against the Tigers, Mickey had 27 in the Yankees first 60 games. For the first 60 games in 1927, the year of the Bambino's record, Ruth had 24. The Babe did not reach the 27 homer mark until his seventy-eighth game of the season on July 8, 1927.

To round out the month of June, Mantle hit home runs from both sides of the plate for the fourth time in his career in the Yankees second game victory over the Senators. The Yankees won the first game by the score of 3-2 and were tied at six-all in the nightcap, when Mickey homered in the seventh for his twenty-eighth of the year swinging right-handed against Dean Stone.

On his next turn at bat, the switch-hitter batting left-handed against Bud Byerly, unloaded number twenty-nine into the bull pen in right field with a mate aboard to win it in sudden death fashion, in the bottom of the ninth for an 8-6 win.

Mel Ott, the former Giant slugger who holds the National League record for home runs with 511, doubts whether Babe Ruth's mark of 60 will be broken by the Yankee's Mantle this year. Ott, now a Detroit Tiger broadcaster, believes Mantle's bad knees may prevent him from playing a full schedule, but he hinted that "pressure" will prove to be the Yankee slugger's biggest handicap. "Mickey seems impatient at the plate; he's going for bad balls and that's going to hurt him," Ott commented.

The comparison of the young and super talented Mantle to Babe Ruth is constantly ongoing. Many Hall of Famers, including Ty Cobb were present at a June gathering by invitation of the Kansas City Athletics to discuss only baseball. Many veterans, while lavishing great praise on the young Mantle, were not ready to place him in the same category as Ruth.

One of the Hall's members stated that "Ruth faced much better pitchers. During the Babe's time the pitchers started what they finished, nowadays there are often four or five pitchers in a game, some of them not so good. I don't know how many homers Babe would hit if he faced the pitching you see today."

Ty Cobb stated simply, "it's too early to make a comparison between Mickey and Ruth. Wait until Mickey has been up there another four or five years. Mantle's young yet."

Pat Collins, who is not a Hall of Famer but was Babe's one-time roommate when Pat did some of the catching for the Yankees, was not shy about supporting the Bambino. "I know Mantle looks great, but we forget Ruth. The Babe had one of the greatest arms in baseball and he was one of the best base runners. Mantle has the advantage only in speed, nothing else. Ruth hit 'em farther. I have to laugh when I read that Mantle hit one farther than Babe. Nobody ever hit them as far as the Babe."

Hall of Famer, Frankie Frisch added a scoffing note: "The one comparison I'd make on this Ruth-Mantle question," he said, "has to do with those silly helmets the players wear these days. Ruth never used one."

By mid-June the Dodgers were beginning to wake up. On Saturday, June 16, Duke Snider clouted his fifteenth homer of the season in the eighth inning to break a 2-2 deadlock, enabling the Bums to defeat the Braves, 3-2. The win was the Dodgers tenth in their last twelve starts.

Perhaps the Dodgers recent success gave them an unfair vote of confidence, as they dropped both ends of a double-header the following day to the Milwaukee club. Bob Buhl picked up his sixth win of the season in a route going performance, as Braves first baseman Joe Adcock slammed two home runs to help the visitors to a 5-4 victory. In the night-cap, Adcock homered again to support the fine pitching of Ray Crone who earned his sixth win and was the victor by the score of 3-1 over Don Newcombe.

Gil Hodges, the fine Dodger first baseman, gained the distinction of being the eighteenth major leaguer to hit 250 or more homers in his career when he connected for a round-tripper off Crone in the nightcap.

The Braves Sunday sweep over the Dodgers attracted 34,394, the largest crowd at Ebbets Field since June of 1951.

Although held to only two hits, the Pirates defeated the Cardinals 2-0 in a contest that was called after seven innings due to rain. Bob Friend, who yielded eight hits in going the distance, picked up his eleventh win of the season. He ran his scoreless innings streak to 27 against the Redbirds, while running his career record against the Cards to 25-8. The Pirates' Lee Walls accounted for both of the Pirates runs in the second inning. After failing on two attempts to bunt, Walls then homered of the Cardinals Herm Wehmeier.

The shift, then and now! When Ted Williams grounded to Frank Bolling in the eighth inning of the June 16 game at Detroit, the Tiger second baseman was playing back so far in right field that he was unable to throw out the Red Sox star. If he had been playing a normal position, he probably would have started a double play. As a result of the play, Tigers manager Bucky Harris revised his defensive alignment for the Splendid Splinter, explaining, "You can't play Williams that deep any more. He used to hit line drives out there and a man in short right was valuable. Now he's hitting them on the ground or all the way to the fence, so the second baseman will have to play in."

While the Red Sox were in the Detroit area, Ted Williams put on a home run-hitting display at Flint, Michigan for the benefit of the city's boys' baseball program, clouting 25 drives over the fences at Flint's Atwood Stadium. The Red Sox star poled several drives over the light towers, 90 feet high and 310 feet from home plate, to the delight of the fans attending. Williams competed with Charley Maxwell of the Tigers, who belted five over the walls, and Jim Piersall of the Red Sox, who socked one, off Mickey Owen, the Bosox coach. The generous major leaguers appeared at the request of one of Williams' former teammates, who now directs the kids' baseball program at Flint. Makes one wonder just how Ted Williams would have fared in the annual Home Run Derby at today's All-Star games?

Red Schoendienst of the Giants and Pee Wee Reese, Carl Erskine and Duke Snider of the Dodgers will compete for a $1,000 prize when they appear on "The Arthur Murray Dance Party" on CBS-TV at 10:00 p.m. on June 28.

Phil Rizzuto, the 37 year old shortstop has been reduced to a bench-warmer role by the Yankees, and will retire from the game only when the Bombers let him go, he said.

"When I'm through with the Yankees, I'll retire," said the Scooter. "The only other way I'd stay in baseball would be if I got a job managing or coaching in the big leagues." Rizzuto, who has looked like his old self at shortstop, was complimented recently on his fine play. "I'm surprised, too," said Phil. "I'm just feeling frisky and it's no strain at all for me to play. Sitting on the bench some has made me less tense and I feel a lot more relaxed than when I played every day."

Rizzuto also said that he had learned something else about himself after all these years. "I kept watching Gil McDougal playing short," he explained, "and it struck me that he took his time, while I always hurried my throws. So I'm taking my time now and it's been a lot easier to avoid errors." It is ironic that Rizzuto would feel this way, because his greatness is the fact that he has always been great on getting the ball away so quickly.

Rabbit ball, tighter round balls, or just bigger, stronger players might account for balls flying over the centerfield fence at Forbes Field. Although no National League player had ever hit a ball over the right-center or center field wall since Forbes Field was built in 1909 until this season started, three accomplished the feat within three weeks.

Dale Long was the first to drop a shot over the right-center wall near the 436-foot sign on the fence, May 23, against the Cardinals. A few days later Duke Snider topped Long's shot with a blast a few feet to the left. And on Sunday, June 17, Stan Musial of the Cardinals became the third in the trio to hit a shot over that wall.

Slugger Dale Long was not only the "talk of the town," he was the "talk of the nation" during his recent consecutive homer streak. Dale signed promptly with Frank Scott the baseball players' representative in New York and his first payoff was an appearance on the Ed Sullivan show, for which the slugger received $500.

Ernie Banks, now in his third season with the Cubs, obviously is on his way to just as fine a season as he had last year. At the end of June he had driven in 47 runs, scored 44, and has collected eleven doubles, four triples and twenty homers.

As the month ended, Banks was two days ahead of his spectacular 44 homer pace of 1955 which enabled him to etch his name into the records as the number one slugging shortstop in major league history.

When Duke Snider hit his seventeenth homer of the season and number 250 of his career, June 29, the Dodger outfielder reached a milestone that teammate Gil Hodges had attained just 12 days earlier, against the Braves.

In the same game that Snider blasted round-tripper number 250, Hodges drove two balls out of the park to increase his lifetime total to 254. It marked the first time in National League history that two players on the same team had hit 250 homers apiece while playing together. The only American Leaguers to do it were Babe Ruth and Lou Gehrig.

Consecutive homers by Snider, Ransom Jackson and Hodges with one out in the ninth inning produced four runs and enabled the Dodgers to edge the Phillies 6-5, in a story book finish. As a result of the victory the boys from Flatbush climbed to within one game of the pace-setting Braves and Reds.

In the bottom of the ninth, Junior Gilliam coaxed a walk off Stu Miller, who had yielded only four hits in the previous eight innings. Pee Wee Reese was retired by Miller, and then Snider socked a four-bagger to drive Miller from the game. He was relieved by Russ Meyer, who promptly gave up back to back home runs to Jackson and Hodges for the Dodger walk-off win. Clem Labine, who had relieved to pitch the ninth, picked up his seventh win of the season against only two losses.

It had been eight years since Gil Hodges had worked behind the plate, when he returned to his old position for two innings and handled the catcher's mitt with his old-time skill. Hodges had shifted to first base in 1948 when the Dodgers obtained Roy Campanella has also spent time in the outfield.

Manager Smokey Alston turned to Hodges for catching duties after Rube Walker was lifted for a pinch-runner and Campanella was ejected for protesting a ball-and-strike call.

With Charlie Maxwell hitting two homers and Al Kaline adding a solo shot, the Tigers defeated the Athletics 5-0, behind the five hit pitching of Billy Hoeft. In a battle of lefties, Hoeft out dueled Tommy LaSorda who was searching for his first win of the season. Instead, LaSorda was tagged with his fourth defeat.

Nothing odd about the fact that Ted Williams and Mickey Mantle were ranked "one-two" in the American League batting race as the month of June came to a close. Williams was hitting .373, while Mantle was at .371 to go with his league leading 29 homers.

In the National League, the St. Louis Cardinals showed their hitting prowess as five of the top NL batters were Redbirds. Gene Smith, Rip Repulski, Ken Boyer, Wally Moon and Stan Musial were among the elite group, with Smith the league leader at .350.

The Braves excellence on the mound shown through as the season neared the mid-point. Four of the top six pitchers statistically were Milwaukee moundsmen, led by Lew Burdette, who was at 8-4 with a league leading 2.29 ERA. Burdette has already fashioned three shutouts. As the Braves were at or near the top of the standings, Ray Crone, Gene Conley and Warren Spahn all boasted ERA's under 3.00.

The end of June also brought a change of policy regarding beer in three major league ballparks. From now on, fans in all three New York ballparks will have to shell out 35 to 40 cents whenever they thirst for beer, because they will not be permitted to bring their own.

By mutual agreement, the Yankees, Giants and Dodgers have imposed a ban against bringing beer in bottles or cans into the parks.

Their reasoning is not to sell more beer at the concession stands, they insist, although that is sure to be a direct benefit of the ban. Instead, officials of the clubs say it is to forestall any bottle or can-throwing incidents which have occurred all too frequently this season in some cities.

Both the Giants and Dodgers have been involved in bottle and debris throwing incidents at Connie Mack Stadium in Philadelphia. The situation there became so serious that Phillies owner, Bob Carpenter had to ask for more police protection.

In Philly and Pittsburgh, no beer is sold in the parks because of a state law, so fans bring their own, frequently in case lots! Taverns near the parks urge the fans to stock up before going to the game and canned beer is sold in special insulated packages to insure that it will remain cold until consumed. After every game there is a litter of bottles and cans in the stands and the temptation occasionally becomes great to hurl the empties onto the field.

On the recent trip of the Yankees to Chicago, numerous bottles, cans and other objects were hurled around Mickey Mantle in center field, and that apparently is what finally spurred the local operators into action.

Thus the general ban was imposed and all beer and soft drinks now consumed at the parks will be served, as in the past, in paper cups. In Brooklyn, the Flatbush faithful often have their grandstand beer parties, using their own paper cups they brought with them.

Yankee Stadium, of course, has its plush clubhouse saloons in which fans who have the proper credentials can indulge on beer and other alcoholic preferences at fancy prices.

Veteran Cubs pitcher, Paul Minner's comment on the lively ball: "Someday a pitcher is gonna bounce a curve ball that will hit the protruding corner of the plate and jump over the center field fence. These balls are different."

Those close to the game wonder about the notion that more homers are being hit because of bigger stronger batters? What about the pitchers? Are they shorter and skinnier? The consensus of opinion is that the players from a couple decades earlier were hitting fewer homers because they were swinging at 'mush balls'!

The Morath Engineering Company of Wilton, Connecticut has been selling bats with gauges inserted in the barrelheads to register miles per hour of a swing. Top Dodgers were Rube Walker, Duke Snider and Clem Labine, and all were clocked at 115 miles per hour. Ted Kluzewski registered 116. The company does not insist that the higher the figure the better the swing, but proposes that each player, when he is swinging just right, establishes his own norm, which should be recorded. Then when the player is in a slump, the meter will tell if he is over swinging or under swinging. "It has a psychological contribution," suggests Big Klu. "At least it gives a slumping batter something tangible to attribute his slump to. Now, all he hears is a bunch of different suggestions, most of them contradictory."

The stuffing of the All-Star ballots by the Cincinnati fans has writers and fans all over the country up in arms. Why not have All-Star ballots handed out at all ball parks, and let the cash customers vote? That would reduce the one-city domination that is occurring this year, and would give the franchise privilege to the persons who deserve it, the ones paying cash at the box office.

Manager Birdie Tebbetts of the Cincinnati Reds hails his

prize All-Star rookie, Frank Robinson, as one of the few ball players he has ever seen who can take a full swing with the bat, then stop the bat short of the plate to avoid being liable for a called strike when he does not believe the pitch is in the strike zone.

"Ted Williams and Stan Musial can do it and so could Joe DiMaggio, to name a few," Tebbetts said. "It takes great strength in the arms and wrists and perfect co-ordination of the mind and muscles to do this and Robinson has it all," Tebbetts added.

Only 4,581 fans were in attendance at Comiskey Park in Chicago on June 21 to witness what is probably the major leagues best overall pitched game of the season. The White Sox behind Jack Harshman defeated the Baltimore Orioles 1-0 in a contest that was played in two hours and twelve minutes. (2:12) Harshman and O's hurler Connie Johnson each pitched a one-hitter, with Harshman only allowing a single hit to Gus Triandos, the O's catcher. Nellie Fox had the Sox only hit and he came around to score the decisive run as Harshman evened his record at 4-4, while Johnson suffered his fourth defeat, to go with his two victories.

With catcher Ed Bailey smashing three homers in the opening game, the Redlegs exploded for six circuit shots to defeat the Dodgers in a doubleheader, 10-6 and 2-1 on Sunday, June 24. Joe Nuxhall pitched a three-hitter in the nightcap, becoming the first lefthander to hurl a route going victory over the Dodgers in Ebbets Field since he did it himself back in 1954. Bailey became the second Redleg batter to hit three dingers in one game this season. Bailey's teammate Gus Bell accomplished the feat earlier against the Cubs.

The upstart Braves set a new club record for most consecutive games won since moving to Milwaukee in 1953 when they scored three runs in the ninth inning to defeat the Phillies 8-5, moving their winning streak to eleven straight. Bobby Thomson had four hits to lead the attack in support of Bob

Buhl's eighth win of the season.

An interesting side note in comparing pace of play in the '56 season to the current 'era of pitch clock baseball,' in the 2019 season. A member of the Kansas City Star's sports staff found only 10 minutes of actual play in a two hour and thirty-eight minute (2:38) contest. A stopwatch was employed to determine just how much actual action a contest of this length involves.

The Athletics battled the Senators, and since the hometown A's won the contest, the duration was for only eight and one half innings and for all this time the ball was in play for only nine minutes and 55 seconds.

A second was allowed for each pitch from the time it left the pitcher's hand until the umpire made his call. Home runs were counted as in play until they left the park and disappeared from sight. That meant that two hours and 28 minutes were used without action.

The results, although done in fun were interesting as compiled by staff writer Dick Wade of the Kansas City Star. He discovered, for example, that pitchers consumed most of this time. Dean Stone, one of the Washington hurlers, used 14 seconds on average between throws. Camilo Pascual required 17 seconds, while Pedro Ramos needed only eight seconds.

Jose Santiago, who was pitching for the A's, took an average of 11 seconds, while Bobby Shantz who pitched the ninth, needed only seven seconds between each pitch.

Batters, too, used a lot of time. Jose Valdivielso, the Nats' shortstop, stepped out of the box between pitches, using up eleven seconds each time.

Wade clocked a relief act on the part of Washington as manager Charlie Dressen yanked Stone. It went this way: Stone and catcher Lou Berberet huddled for 20 seconds, Stone and second baseman Pete Runnels discussed things for 18 seconds. Stone left and Pascual came in, then, Pascual, Berberet, the catcher and Dressen mulled over the situation for one minute and ten seconds. It then took 22 seconds for Pascual to warm up and for the umpire to brush off home plate and signal play to start. (Ernest Mehl)

As a staunch supporter of baseball, this writer firmly believes that batters stepping out of the plate nowadays on almost every pitch to adjust their batting gloves, along with the numerous pitching changes are the things that slow the pace of play the most! Of course, each and every MLB game is now televised with the commercials paying the way for our viewing pleasure, and doing more than their share to add time to games. Players enjoy their time on the television screen, and stepping out guarantees more "face time."

Quite simply, games played in the 1956 season were rarely televised, thus it is easy to see how games of 'the pitch clock era' can take up to thirty minutes or more than those of yesteryear!

Not a problem, as a baseball purist, I love when the game goes three hours-plus, anyway!

Mickey Mantle's two homers at Briggs Stadium provided a perfect excuse for a man hauled into a Detroit court on drunkenness charges, June 21. After the individual insisted he was at the ball park rather than in a saloon, Judge John Scalion asked him for the score of the game. He failed to come up with the exact score, but described exactly where the Yankees star's homers had gone and the charges were dismissed.

Much is being made in baseball circles about Braves Manager Fred Haney shaking hands with and congratulating Robin Roberts after the Phillies great pitcher had stopped Milwaukee's 11-game winning streak. Some people around baseball feel this is not in line with true competition.

Haney, who was coaching third base when Roberts ended the game by striking out Eddie Mathews, walked toward the right-hander and offered a handshake. "I have never had an opposing player or the opposing manager to shake my hand because I had just beaten his team," said Roberts. "I thought it was a nice gesture and I appreciated it."

Haney wasn't expressing joy over losing all he did was prove that he has the capacity to take a crushing defeat like a man. A congratulatory handshake seems to be traditional in American sports, professional as well as amateur. Rivals do it in sports like basketball, football, boxing, as well as the more gentlemanly forms of competition like golf and tennis. Isn't it time that the great game of baseball, follows suit? (Lloyd Larson, Milwaukee Sentinel)

You can't convince Early Wynn, the burly Indians' pitcher, that Ted Williams doesn't do his own umpiring. During two successive games in Boston, Wynn howled in anger when his pitches to Williams were called balls. Wynn is still certain the pitches he bitterly complained about were strikes. "One," he says, "couldn't have been any more perfect, right down the middle."

Mel Harder, the Indians' pitching coach, agrees with Wynn that a reputation helps the hitter. Says Harder: "In my day, Babe Ruth always got five strikes. Once a player gets a reputation for having a 'great eye,' he is soon umpiring his own game."

Casey Stengel, a man of a few thousand words, tells why Mickey Mantle is growing up to be one of the game's greatest players ever. Stengel will describe by the hour Mantle's natural power at the plate, and for another hour Mickey's speed on the bath paths and in the outfield. Then if you are still with him, Casey will go into Mantle's over-all quickness and co-ordination.

Whether his wanderings take him to Tokyo or to Brooklyn, Stengel has never needed an interpreter because he speaks 'Stengelese,' a language which is his own.

Typical of Stengel comments on his star center fielder is one that involves Mickey's improved fielding. "Didn't you think he made a great catch on the fellow in Chicago?" asks Casey, who finds it hard to remember names. "The ball was hit past him and he just caught up with it. And he did it against that Kileen (Kaline) in Detroit, too, all the way out to the flag pole in center."

Stengel tells how he first took an interest in the shy Mantle when the youth reported to the Yankees. "The first thing I had to teach Mantle was to run in the outfield, which DiMaggio was so great at, and not run looking down at the ground." Casey continued, "They have no plowed fields up here, boy,' I tell him, 'and you don't have to run and watch out for the furrows or cow piles at the same time because this is the big leagues and the fields're all level and they have groundskeepers and everything.' So now he does that and makes catches which would surprise you." (Tom Meany)

The Minor Leagues
(Down on the Farm)

Satchel Paige's old habit of showing up late for departures put the ancient hurler in the Miami Marlins' doghouse, when he missed the chartered plane carrying the club to Rochester early on the morning of June 11.

"I overslept," the veteran pitcher explained to General Manager Eddie Stumpf. "It won't happen again, I promise."

The GM was inclined to believe the explanation, but nevertheless made Satchel plunk down his own money for passage on a commercial airliner.

American Association spectators in Indianapolis were treated to the unusual sight of a "pinch-runner running for a pinch-runner" in a contest with the Denver Bears. In the eighth inning of the contest, after Ron Northey was issued a base on balls by Denver pitcher Ed Maier, Manager Kerby Farrell inserted Ed Gasque as a replacement runner for Northey. Gasque had hardly touched first base when Farrell changed his mind and sent in Roger Maris.

On June 6, the Denver club played without the services

of second baseman Bobby Richardson, who received permission to go to his home in Sumter, South Carolina to be married to Miss Alice Elizabeth Dobson

The San Antonio Missions of the Texas League hammered five home runs to take a twin-bill from the Shreveport club, 17-4 and 5-4 on June 11. In the opener, Brooks Robinson clubbed two homers, while in the nightcap Gene Oden slammed a round-tripper with a mate aboard in the ninth inning to turn apparent defeat into victory.

Since 1952, the Hollywood Stars of the Pacific Coast League have had a corner on the Rookie of the Year market. Nineteen year old Bill Mazeroski is a leading candidate to make it five straight for the Stars in 1956.

Only in his third year as a pro, and the son of a West Virginia coal miner, Mazeroski broke in with Williamsport of the Eastern League in 1954 as a 17 year old. His initial season was good enough to earn Bill a tryout with the Stars, a Pittsburgh farm, in the spring of '55.

"Bill's the best second baseman in the league, bar none," said Colonel Clay Hopper, the man who steers the Stars.

Bill had been a shortstop, but switched to second base at Branch Rickey's suggestion. He was in too deep when the '55 season opened and hit only .170. He was shipped back to Williamsport, where he hit .291.and played superb defensively.

Observers who saw the kid in '55 found it hard to believe that this was the same fellow. The acrobatic kid had one string of 27 errorless games and but for a single error, would have had a string up in the forties.

Mazeroski says he gained a lot of confidence playing in the Dominican Republic last winter. He also gained a lot of weight, as he was 15 pounds heavier and had grown a couple inches when he reported this spring.

Lefty O'Doul, the Vancouver manager, predicts that Steve Bilko will come closer to breaking the PCL homer record of 60, set by Tony Lazzeri, than Mickey Mantle will cracking

Babe Ruth's major loop mark of 60. Bilko has 28 as of June 19. More than a home run hitter, Bilko won a steak dinner for two, offered by the Angels when he became the first player to reach the century mark in base hits. He extended his personal game hitting streak to 23.

More of the shameful sign of the times! The Texas League, which has permitted use of Negro players the past five seasons, was faced with a new racial problem if a bill passed by the Louisiana House of Representatives is enacted into law.

Under a segregation bill approved by the body, no athletic contests involving mixed races would be permitted in Louisiana. The sponsor of the bill later said he would not object to an amendment to permit Shreveport to play against Negroes in the Texas League for the remainder of the season. There is speculation that a bar on the appearance of Negroes could eventually force Shreveport out of the league.

Outfielder Yale Lary has joined the Austin Senators of the Texas League following completion of a two year military hitch. However, the former Texas A & M star and NFL All-Pro plans to leave the club in mid-July to begin training for one more season of pro football with the Detroit Lions. Lary, later was to become a member of the NFL's 1950's All-Decade team and was elected to the NFL Hall of Fame in 1979.

Denver Bears infielder, Tony Kubek hit safely in 15 consecutive games before his streak was stopped by Charleston's Dick Marlowe on June 16.

Just two nights earlier in Denver, the appearance of comedian Max Patkin helped bring out 7,392 fans. Rain interrupted the game several times as the Bears defeated Louisville 20-6. Bobby Richardson led the attack with two homers and six RBIs. Ralph Terry pitched the distance to record his sixth win in seven decisions.

The same Bobby Richardson hit safely in 12 consecutive games before being stopped by Hank Aguirre, Indianapolis southpaw on June 27.

Stricter adherence to the curfew rules may be expected from International League teams when visiting Miami, as a result of the experience of three Montreal Royals who went out on the town. The Royals Dixie Howell, who is a catcher and coach along with pitchers Billy Harris and Robert Walz were fined an aggregate of $100 in Miami Beach Police Court after being arrested at 4:00 a.m., June 19 for their involvement in a night club rhubarb..

Howell's penalty was not limited to the fine either, as Buzzy Bavasi, Brooklyn Dodgers vice-president and the president of the Royals, announced the catcher-coach was suspended indefinitely.

Blanked twelve times in a row by the Cubans' shift, former major leaguer Luke Easter finally broke loose against the Sugar Kings, June 14, with a homer and two singles for his biggest night in a Bison uniform.

Rocky Colavito, touted as possibly the strongest throwing outfielder in the game today, failed to break the Organized Baseball long distance throwing record. The Cleveland-owned outfielder, recently sent here to San Diego on option, heaved one throw 435 feet, ten inches from the plate over the center-field wall at Lane Field for his best effort in the pregame exhibition.

The throw was slightly more than seven feet short of the record 433 feet, set by Don Grate at Chattanooga of the Southern League in 1953.

The Class A Sally League is getting a real summer treat as Harmon Killebrew has arrived. Killebrew, who was sent to Charlotte by Washington at the expiration of his bonus tenure, celebrated his twentieth birthday by clouting a two-run homer in a 5-2 triumph over Knoxville, June 29, four days after he joined the Hornets. Two nights earlier, the young third sacker walloped a grand-slam homer in the opening frame. He received a birthday cake from his former skipper, Chuck Dressen.

Cincinnati Redleg fans, even in Charleston, West Virginia accept defeat of their favorites very bitterly, it was revealed recently. When a woman appeared at police headquarters in Charleston and demanded a felonious assault warrant for the arrest of her husband on the grounds that he had struck her several times, the lieutenant asked, "Why did he hit you?" "Because those Redlegs got beat," was the answer. The hubby was jailed and missed hearing the radio description of the Reds' twin-bill sweep over the Cardinals.

Tempers which flared on the field during a Southwestern League game in Hobbs, New Mexico, cooled off behind bars in the city jail. Three players spent the night in "the pokey."

Following a loud and red-hot exchange of words in the first inning between a Hobbs batter and a Clovis pitcher, the two players squared off in a battle of fists. Hobbs police broke it up and took the two belligerents off to jail. After the game, the police returned to the park and took Clovis Third Baseman Jackie Wilcox into custody. Wilcox was arrested because he had been abusive to the police.

The players were released on bond the next morning and they were let off with a stern lecture by the city judge.

The arresting officers said they stepped in because some of the players had been using profane language within the hearing of many of the 700 fans in the park. (Art Gatts)

CHAPTER FOUR

All-Stars, Awards and Rhubarbs
(Standings as of July 1, 1956)

American League				National League			
Team	**W**	**L**	**GB**	**Team**	**W**	**L**	**GB**
New York	46	25	---	Milwaukee	37	26	---
Chicago	39	26	4	Cincinnati	39	28	---
Cleveland	39	29	5 ½	Brooklyn	38	29	1
Boston	35	32	9	St. Louis	36	33	4
Baltimore	32	38	13 ½	Pittsburgh	32	35	7
Detroit	30	37	14	Philadelphia	29	39	10 ½
Washington	29	45	18 ½	New York	28	38	10 ½
Kansas City	26	44	19 ½	Chicago	26	37	11

Cincinnati pitcher, Brooks Lawrence kept the Redlegs near the top of the National League race as the mid-season approached. The big right-hander, obtained in a trade with the St. Louis Cardinals just before the beginning of the season had a brilliant first half, posting a 13-0 record, and was named to the NL All-Star team.. He tailed off later in the season, but would finish the year with a 19-10 record.

Bob Friend of the Pittsburgh Pirates, who many recognized as the best pitcher in baseball, kept the lowly Pirates on the brink of contention with an 11-5 mark at the half-way point. Friend was brilliant, he made 42 starts, threw 314 innings, which included 19 complete games, and had a 3.46 ERA on the way to a 17-17 record and he too, was named to the NL All-Star team.

The previous season ('55), Friend became the first pitcher ever to lead the league in ERA, while pitching for a last place club. He had a 14-9 record with an astonishing 2.83 ERA.

From 1951-65, a 15 year stretch, Bob Friend won 191 games for the Pirates, including an 18 win season with the Bucs when they won the World Series title in 1960. Overall, he won 197 major league games, often with a second division club.

Bob Friend, recognized as one of the true gentlemen in the game, passed away in 2019.

The Sporting News, recognized world-wide as the Baseball Newspaper of the World, presented their first Player of the Decade Award to Stan Musial of the St. Louis Cardinals. Musial, the six-time National League batting champion and winner of three Most Valuable Player Awards was presented the award just prior to the All-Star Game.

The presentation was made by Bob Feller, who had suggested to The Sporting News that they name a player of the decade, chosen by sports writers, sportscasters, players, club officials and umpires.

Essentially, the selection amounted to a three-way battle between Musial, Joe DiMaggio and Ted Williams. All three basically are outfielders, but Musial in addition to playing different outfield positions also plays some first base. Over 260 observers were in on the selection of the nation's top players from 1946-55. The award, presented by Feller to Musial was a grandfather clock.

Stan "The Man" when informed of his selection for the Player of the Decade Award was greatly impressed. "I don't know of anything except Hall of Fame selection that could please me so much," he remarked. "I say that because I'm so highly flattered to have been chosen when, as the list shows, there were so many great players to choose from. I'm fortunate the ten years covered my peak seasons."

Ralph Kiner, now the General Manager at San Diego after a lengthy career of hitting home runs for Pittsburgh, Chicago and Cleveland said he regarded it "practically impossible" to separate his first four, Feller, Williams, Musial and DiMaggio.

During the ten year period, while boosting his lifetime average to .342 and his salary to $80,000 per year, Musial batted consecutively .365, .312, .376, .338, .346, .355, .336, .337, .330 and .319.

Bob Broeg of the St. Louis Post-Dispatch seemed to sum it up best when he stated, "The ten-year period, if adhered to strictly, is Musial's."

All eyes were on the All-Star Game, to be played in Griffith Stadium in Washington, D. C., on Tuesday, July 10. The twenty-third mid-summer classic would feature many future Hall of Fame players, and would be viewed by a capacity crowd of 28,587, with the first pitch at 1:00 p.m.

The Mutual Broadcasting System, consisting of some 560 stations, broadcast the classic. Armed Forces Radio Service aired the game worldwide by short wave radio to occupation troops overseas and to Naval ships at sea. Bob Wolfe of the Washington Senators and Bob Neal of the "Mutual Game of the Day," handled the broadcast.

The National Broadcasting Company (NBC) with the Gillette Razor Company as the chief sponsor televised the game nationwide, with Mel Allen of the Yankees and Al Hefler of the Dodgers handling the telecasts.

The rabid Cincinnati voters were in control, as their beloved Redlegs continued to bounce in and out of first place. There seemed to be many flaws in the voting and Cincinnati radio station WSAI played a major part in determining the make-up of the National League squad. With eight Cincinnati players on the NL All-Star squad of 25, this was the first year in a long time the Redlegs have so many favorites picked.

None of the Reds became peeved over the criticism directed at them in the East because of their selection for the All-Star squad. "It's a free country and anyone who thinks we don't belong on that team has a right to say so. But we think we belong on it," is the way they brushed off their detractors.

Commissioner Ford Frick admitted there were flaws in the poll, with the inordinate weight Radio Station WSAI in Cincinnati had in determining the five Redleg players in the NL starting lineup. The WSAI campaign for backing the Redlegs fueled speculation that they provided one-third of the total ballots. Frick discussed "the last minute rush from Cincinnati was indeed an unsatisfactory factor," he said, "but I am not too disturbed about it." He continued, "every single vote was legitimate, the WSAI totals were investigated and verified."

The controversy continued as Will Harridge, president of the American League stated, "it is very likely that we will go back to having the 16 managers select the teams as they did in the first few years the game was played."

Sportswriters chimed in with their own opinions. Max Kase, a New York writer suggested, "Five Reds on the NL team stresses the importance of a need for a different selection process. The big Rhineland vote was brought out by smart promotion, but it hardly reflects the fan sentiment on the national level."

Ed McAuley of the Cleveland News stated, "This year's election produced evidence that not all fans are superbly qualified. One voter tried three times to spell 'Schoendienst,' finally gave up and made it 'Gilliam.' Another voted for Ralph Kiner, who is now the general manager at San Diego. But I hope the authorities leave the franchise to the customers. They make their mistakes, but the managers did no better when they picked the teams. Remember the year they left off a shortstop named Lou Boudreau?"

Personally, this writer remembers vividly scratching out several All-Star ballots of my own that summer, and mailing them in similar fashion, as I, too was guilty of "ballot stuffing," voting for numerous St. Louis Cardinals on each of the ballots I entered. Postage for a letter in 1956 was a mere three cents!

With no starters from last season's world's champion Dodgers, none from the Cubs, Braves, Giants or Phillies, the National League coasted to a 7-3 win in the twenty-third All-Star Game.

"What was all the squawking about?" asked Redlegs manager, Birdie Tebbetts. "The only reason that Cincinnati had so many players on the All-Star team was because they happen to be the best players in the National League. Maybe nobody noticed it, but at the time of the All-Star Game, Cincinnati happened to be in first place."

Here's how the Redleg players fared: Frank Robinson went 0 for 2, Johnny Temple, two singles in four at-bats, and had the only stolen base of the game. Ted Kluszewski, two for two, both doubles, Roy McMillan, two for three, Ed Bailey, no hits in his three at-bats and Gus Bell no hits in one at-bat. Big Klu and Temple each had an RBI. In fifteen at-bats, the Redleg players had six hits, for a batting average of .400 for the game.

Ken Boyer of the St. Louis Cardinals was the real heart breaker for the American League, as he hit safely in his first three trips to the plate. But, it was in the field that Boyer really broke the AL hearts. He started with the AL leadoff hitter, Harvey Kuenn in the first inning. Kuenn drilled Bob Friend's first pitch for an apparent single into left field, but Boyer dove to his left and somehow caught the ball as he sprawled on the ground. In the fifth inning, Boyer again picked on Kuenn. This time Harvey rammed a liner down the left field foul line for what would be an apparent double. Boyer hurled himself to the right and managed to knock down the ball, and was up instantly with the ball in his hand and fired to first baseman Dale Long to retire Kuenn for the second time.

Recognized as two of the best plays ever in All-Star play, Boyer wasn't done yet, as he leaped into the air to grab a liner off Pinch-Hitter Ray Boone's bat for the third out of the seventh inning.

There were numerous other National League standouts, the Giants' Willie Mays, who bashed a two-run homer and scored a second run on a wild dash around the bases; Stan Musial, Player of the Decade, who hit his fifth All-Star homer in his thirteenth game, and the starting and finishing pitchers Bob Friend of the Pirates and Johnny Antonelli of the Giants. But the real sizzler in the game was Ken Boyer.

Trailing 5-0 in the sixth inning, the American Leaguers made some noise. Nellie Fox opened the inning with a single off Warren Spahn, the outstanding Milwaukee southpaw. Ted Williams, who had left two runners on base with a weak ground-out in the third, brought the crowd to its feet with a long home run into the center field bull pen.

The home town American League fans were still yelling when Mickey Mantle, a victim of three strikeouts, banged another homer into the left field bleachers, cutting the NL lead to 5-3. National League manager, Walt Alston relieved Spahn, who had pitched well in the fourth and fifth inning and replaced him with Antonelli. The Giants' lefty promptly gave up singles to Sherm Lollar and Al Kaline before getting Vic Power on a fly-out and inducing George Kell to roll into a double-play grounder to McMillan at short. The American League was done!

While both teams had eleven hits, with two homers for each side, and both teams played errorless ball, the National Leaguers looked better at the plate, in the field, on the bases and on the mound. The NL pitchers did not walk a single batter, while the AL issued four bases on balls, with two of those free passes turning into runs.

Bob Friend who hurled three scoreless innings was the winning pitcher, while ChiSox lefty, Billy Pierce took the loss, allowing only one run in his three innings of work. Although Antonelli gave up four hits, he closed strong. After the two singles by Lollar and Kaline, Antonelli retired the last ten batters of the game.

The 7-3 victory and the outstanding performance of the Redleg players in the game, more than vindicated the judgement of the fans that picked the Redleg-studded lineup. (Frederick G. Lieb)

The world champion Dodgers were conspicuous by their absence from the starting NL lineup. This marked the first time since 1939 that a Dodger had not appeared in the opening lineup.

Here's an oddity: Both starting pitchers in the game (Friend and Pierce) wore uniform number 19.

The Hillerich & Bradsby Company, makers of the Louisville Slugger bats, took excellent care of the players, putting two bats in the locker of each of the stars before the game.

National League President, Warren Giles told Walt Alston, "Blame me for the fact that all of the stars did not get to play. I told Walt that the All-Star Game is a contest and not an exhibition game and that he should handle his team just like he would the Dodgers during the season." I pointed out that if he got out in front and wanted to protect his lead that he should use the men he felt were the best defensively. I talked to the players, too and explained that it was an honor to be here, but we are here to win and do not feel bad if you don't get into the game."

Giles continued, "In the early years of the All-Star Game, the National League was treating it as an exhibition and we were getting licked regularly before we woke up."

Ted Williams pointed out in pre-game practice that he had never seen Friend pitch before. "He looked far different than

I imagined." Williams said later, "He's quite a pitcher. He never showed me a fast ball, threw all breaking stuff." Friend fanned Williams on his first trip and got him to roll to first baseman Dale Long with two on and two out in the third inning.

Half an hour before game time, 500 standing-room tickets were placed on sale. Officials made the decision to sell these additional pasteboards in a last- minute session. They were limited to two per customer.

The day before the game, the United States Senate declared a recess until July 11 because of the game. At the same time, the House scheduled a noon session for July 10, with the understanding that it would be completed as quickly as possible. The idea was to give all an opportunity to attend the All-Star Game.

One of the day's biggest cheers from the fans went up in the ninth inning when Roy Sievers, the only Senator on the AL roster, pinch hit for Early Wynn. Sievers, who said before the game that appearing in his first All-Star game was the biggest thrill of his career, popped out. When reporters reached the AL clubhouse after the game, they were treated to a unique sight. Ted Williams, bat in hand, was giving Sievers a hitting lesson. Williams said he had been impressed by Roy's obvious hitting power, but had noted a slight fault which he was trying to correct.

A Cy Young Memorial Award for the outstanding pitcher of the year, a plan strongly favored by Commissioner Ford Frick, was approved at a special meeting of the Baseball Writers' Association of America held in the Statler Hotel, the evening before the All-Star Game. The award will become effective beginning with this season. Only one pitcher will be chosen from the two major leagues, and a hurler will be eligible to win the award only one time!

Much is being said and many meetings are being held regarding a new pension plan for players and former players.

With the pensions starting at age 50, it will be confession time for many players who will revert to their actual ages, instead of their "baseball" years. There was the time Duke Snider, in route from the Coast to Florida, stopped off to see Preacher Roe. Preach greeted Snider with: "Just in time to celebrate my fortieth birthday." Duke spoke in amazement, "Why last year you were 36," he said. "You know how it is," Roe smiled. (Oscar Ruhl)

Pittsburgh Pirate executives hope to do something about eliminating the suspended second games of Sunday doubleheaders at Forbes Field due to the Pennsylvania curfew law that makes it illegal to play ball after 7:00 p.m. on Sundays in the state. They hope to cut down the time between games to the bare minimum of 20 minutes in an effort to add a few minutes to the nightcap and possibly finish the game.

The Pirates already have been involved in two suspended games at Forbes Field. They played off the May 13 contest on July 3 and have a date on August 10 to finish the game of July 1 with the Giants. The game with the Phils had been halted with two out in the Phils' eighth inning. In the contest with the Giants, there is one inning remaining. (Les Biederman)

Warren Spahn's 5-0 whitewashing over the Cubs on July 6 was the Braves lefty's third shutout of the season and thirty-seventh of his illustrious career.

With the Yankees having played exactly half of their regular season games at the All-Star break, Mickey Mantle's numbers were incredible. The Mick, on his way to the Triple Crown, was leading the AL in hitting at a .371 clip, had 102 hits, 29 homers and seventy-one RBIs.

Redlegs manager, Birdie Tebbetts believes rival NL pitchers are making a "clay pigeon" out of his rookie outfielder, Frank Robinson. "They've hit him with pitched balls twelve times this season," Birdie pointed out. "The reason, because they've got the idea that the way to get Frank out is to pitch inside to him. Robinson's answer is a .313 batting average and

18 homers on this inside pitching."

After Jack Hand, Tiger clubhouse man, had placed all the team's "home" uniforms in the center of the clubhouse floor and kicked them thoroughly, "to drive out the evil spirits," the Bengals took the field and beat Cleveland 13-7. They had gone almost three weeks without a home field win. During the drought, the Tigers had lost 14 games and tied one at Briggs Stadium.

Although the Cincinnati Redlegs throughout the years as baseball's oldest franchise have fielded 82 different teams and called on more than 400 pitchers, Brooks Lawrence became the first Cincinnati hurler to win his first 12 decisions in a season when he earned the win over the Cardinals in early July. (Lee Allen)

Robin Roberts became the first National League pitcher to lose ten games this season when he dropped a 2-1 decision to the Dodgers, July 6. Since he had only eight victories at the All-Star Game break, it appeared likely that the Phils' ace might have difficulty winning 20 for the seventh consecutive year.

Starting on July 12, the Redlegs faced the task of playing at least one game on each of 46 consecutive dates. The original schedule gave them three open dates, during that 46 day stretch, but each of those dates has now been filled with the playoff of a postponed game. With so many dates to play in various cities, it may necessitate some air travel for the Cincinnati club.

The Reds are scheduled to play 53 games on those 46 dates, 14 of them to be played in seven double-headers.

Only the Cubs, with 54 games to play on the first 46 playing dates following the All-Star break, were scheduled for more work than the Redlegs during that stretch. However, the schedule gave the Cubs four complete off-days with 12 double-headers among the 54 games they were slated to play. (Tom Swope)

The White Sox vs. Cubs exhibition for the benefit of boys' baseball in the Chicago area, scheduled for August 13, will start at 7:45 p.m., instead of the previously scheduled 8:30 p.m. start to permit the Sox to catch a train for Kansas City where they play the following day.

The crowd of 44,859 at the Polo Grounds for the Giants-Dodgers double-header of July 4 was the largest in the National League since June 20, 1954 when 51,464 jammed the park to see the Giants beat the Brooklyn's 4-3 in 13 innings.

Proud to say that this writer was in the Polo Grounds on July 4, 1956 as a 16 year old, along with several friends for this double-header.

Willie Mays had 27 homers at the All-Star break in 1955, but only 13 this year. However, the super talented Mr. Mays had 19 steals in 20 attempts.

The rumor mill abounds. According to legendary Sportscaster Harry Wismer, Bob Feller will replace Al Lopez as manager of the Indians at the close of the season unless the Tribe wins the 1956 American League pennant. Lopez has won one pennant since becoming the Indians manager in 1951. "Not about to happen," said Feller, responding to the comment.

In the first game of the double-header on July 8, Ted Williams had another big day, as the Splendid Splinter added another milestone to his outstanding career. In the first game the Red Sox hammered the Orioles by the score of 9-0, as Williams hit a homer, double and two singles and included a bases loaded walk that drove in his fourth run of the game. Ted hit career home run number 399 in the first inning to give Frank Sullivan all the runs he needed for his eighth win of the season. The Splinter did all his damage in five innings and retired to the bench after the bases loaded walk.

In the nightcap, the Sox defeated the Orioles 8-4, behind two RBIs from both Billy Goodman and Mickey Vernon. Williams drove in run number 1,500 of his career with a single in the third inning for the BoSox There have been only eleven other players in the history of the major leagues that have had as many RBIs. George Kell, the Oriole third baseman was four for four in the nightcap, and was responsible for all the Oriole runs with two homers and four runs batted in.

It seemed as if nobody wanted to buy or trade for Mel Parnell this year. The Red Sox southpaw was on the block after two seasons during which he could win but five games.

Yes, it was hard to believe that Parnell, who has suffered from a fractured forearm, a wrenched knee and a badly sprained ankle, would be the first left-hander to pitch a no-hit, no run game in Fenway Park.

Parnell, who only walked two batters in the 4-0 masterpiece over the White Sox, made it look simple. Only two balls were hit hard. The first one was a sailing liner into center field by Luis Aparicio which Jimmy Piersall almost misjudged and wound up making a good catch of the ball over his head. The other was a line drive by Minnie Minoso right at third baseman, Billy Klaus.

Through eight innings, Parnell faced only 24 men, the minimum for that distance. In the ninth he opened by walking Sammy Esposito on a 3-2 pitch. It enabled the White Sox to have one runner left on base during the game and as it turned out, it was the best break Mel got.

Luis Apparicio slapped a roller which just eluded Parnell. It rolled close to second base, where second baseman, Billy Goodman was near the bag and had to dive for the ball. He came up with it cleanly and flipped it to Don Buddin for a force play. If there hadn't been a runner on first, Goodman may never have retired Aparicio at first and official scorer Bob Holbrook would have had to record it as a base hit.

With two outs, the last batter would be Walt Dropo, a former teammate. "I was glad it was Big Drop," stated Parnell after the game. "When Walt hit the ball right back at me, I was sure I could beat him to the bag." Mel swooped up Dropo's grounder, raced over to first base, stepped on it for the final putout and shoved the ball in his pocket for safe keeping.

When asked if he knew he had a no-hitter going, Parnell quipped, "Let's not kid about it, I knew it all the time. I don't think anybody pitching doesn't know he's got a chance for a no-hitter. But, I wasn't concerned about the no-hitter, I wanted to win." (Hy Hurwitz)

Ted Williams entered the exalted circle of 400-homer hitters at Fenway Park on the night of July 17 to give Bob Porterfield a 1-0 win over the Kansas City Athletics.

When Ted crossed home plate, he looked up at the press box and pursed his lips as if to spit. He just sneered for an instant, but didn't let go with the saliva. It was just a gentle reminder to his writing friends that he isn't washed up. Ted admitted he wanted to spit, but was afraid he would hit Mickey Vernon, who was in the on deck circle.

Williams has been bothered all season with a severe instep injury and had appeared in 20 games as a pinch-hitter. "It was a long time coming," said Ted. "I didn't think I'd ever get it. This is one of my biggest thrills." He ranked it alongside his ninth-inning home run in the 1941 All-Star Game in Detroit.

Manager Bill Rigney of the Giants disclosed at Milwaukee, July 19 that he had fined Willie Mays $25 for failing to run out a pop-up at St. Louis, but said later that he had returned the money to Willie. Rigney, in revealing the fine, said it had been remitted "because Willie has been hustling since then."

At breakfast the other morning, Chico Fernandez of the Dodgers was chatting in Spanish with his roomie, Sandy Amoros. Don Newcombe, also at the table, took it for about five minutes, then put down his fork and declared: "Dammit, speak English. You might say something about me, and I want to know what it is."

Commissioner Ford Frick, discussing the Boudreau shift on Mickey Mantle: "They used to try the same thing on Babe Ruth, and I can still see the Babe punching a ball to left, trotting two bases and standing on second with his belly quivering as he laughed right in their faces. That's the difference between Mantle and Ruth." (Dick Young)

Milwaukee pitcher, Lew Burdette is often described as "nervous as a cat" on the mound. The best ball player's description of Burdette's fidgeting on the mound: "He'd make coffee nervous."

Don Larsen, who hasn't beaten the Indians in four years, was given another shot at them on July 14, but lasted only three and two-third innings. Tommy Byrne, who relieved with the score 3-0 against the Yankees, held the Tribe to a lone run the rest of the way and eventually won the decision, 5-4. Larsen has not pitched a complete game, incidentally since April.

Washington right-hander Connie Grob, threw just one ball to become the winning pitcher in the Nats 12-11 decision over the Tigers. Grob entered the game with two out and the bases loaded after the Tigers had scored five runs for an 11-7 lead. On Grob's first pitch, Bill Tuttle the runner on third tried to steal home, but was tagged out by Catcher Lou Berberet.

Grob was lifted for a pinch-hitter in the bottom of the eighth, when the Senators rallied for five runs to take the lead. Since Grob was the pitcher of record when his team took the lead, he was credited with the victory.

The Yankees ten and one-half game lead over the second place Indians on the morning of July 16 was the longest advantage the American League pacesetters have held since September of 1953, when they topped the field by the same margin.

Although they continue to struggle to escape the cellar in the National League, the Chicago Cubs have a bright spot in Shortstop Ernie Banks. A check through the NL record book reveals that Banks holds the Cubs all-time record for consecutive games played. The game of July 17 was number

399 in a row for Banks since he broke into the Cubs lineup in September of 1953, which is also the major league all-time record for consecutive games played after first appearing in a lineup.

All of his opponents look alike to Bob Rush, the Cubs' strong-armed right-hander. Bob's first seven wins of the season were over seven different clubs. He didn't notch a repeat victory over a club until July 14, when he whipped the Pirates for the second time for win number eight.

Stan Musial's double in the ninth inning of the nightcap, his seventh hit in nine trips for the day, July 15, represented hit number 100 for the season and enabled the Cardinal slugger to take over the league batting lead, giving him a .327 average.

Probably the greatest Sunday in Stan's history occurred on May 2, 1954 when he set a major league record for home runs in a double-header with five.

Robin Roberts posted his first shutout of the season with a four-hit performance, pitching the Phillies to a 2-0 victory over the Redlegs in the fastest played game in the league this season, only one hour and 38 minutes. (1:38)

Charlie Silvera, third-string Yankee catcher, behind Yogi Berra and Elston Howard, is one of the most popular personalities in the game, and here's an illustration why: American League President Will Harridge received a thank-you note from Silvera "for the real honor paid to me by naming me to the All-Star squad this year as batting practice catcher."

The National League used 47 pitchers in seven games on July 15, a major league record for hurlers working in seven contests in one day.

When the largest Milwaukee County Stadium crowd of the season, 41,118, turned out for the Dodger-Braves twi-night double-header, July 15, the parking lot set its' own record with 10,700 cars parked. A damp note was added, however, when many of them were marooned for hours by rain that washed out the scheduled second game and flooded the lot. At least 20 of the vehicles were in water up to their seats.

Pennant fever is rising in Milwaukee as the Braves pitching staff has played a key role in the surge of manager Fred Haney's athletes.

Joe Adcock's recent home run streak made the headlines, and deservedly so. However, so torrid has been Henry Aaron's recent swing tempo that the young Mobile, Alabama native has made Milwaukee's baseball fans give much of the credit to the youngster. Young Aaron has contributed plenty with his bat, and from the All-Star break moving forward, he has been the most consistent hitter in the league.

Early in the season, Aaron was hitting an embarrassing .167, but since the All-Star break has seen his average soar to well above the .300 mark.

Henry had received a letter from his wife back home, to "not come home unless you are hitting above .300." Naturally, the threat was made in jest, but Henry, never one to take any chances, suddenly began to turn on the steam.

"Whether I'm hitting good or not depends on my timing." Aaron explains, "I never have any trouble seeing the ball. I can't even say I see it better when I'm hitting good or when I'm not. When my timing is off, I have trouble and when it ain't, I don't."

Should the young phenom, whose batting style has been compared to that of Rogers Hornsby, get his talented hand on the batting crown, he will have completed an incredible leap from the softball diamonds of his native Mobile. Henry batted cross-handed as a softball player and still swung with that unorthodox grip later as a member of the Indianapolis Clowns in the Negro American League.

Aaron, who came from a large family, still contributes a good chuck of money for support back home and is helping to send a younger sister through college.

Batting cross-handed with the Clowns, he was swatting the

horsehide at a .380 clip when Braves scout Dewey Griggs came along and stole him from under the noses of the New York Giants.

Young Aaron has been with the Milwaukee club not quite three seasons and already a growing legend has been started about the 22 year-old youngster in the hottest baseball town in America.

His hitting style is so relaxed that Robin Roberts once said "Aaron sleeps between pitches."

With his amazing wrist-action and whiplash power, to go along with a remarkable batting eye, observers believe that he will in the not too distant future consistently outhit Willie Mays. Remarkably strong for his size, he's only five feet, 11 and has a wiry, 175 pound frame. Henry pays "no mind" to all the accolades about what he can do. Mention the word "hit" and young Aaron's eyes just about pop out of his head. (Lou Chapman)

Although Mickey Mantle smashed his thirty-first homer of the season, as well as a triple and single, the Yankees had their 11 game winning streak snapped when they lost both games of a double-header to the Tigers in Yankee Stadium on Wednesday, July 18.

In the nightcap, Al Kaline led the Tigers to a 4-3 win, by homering in the sixth inning and then saved the game in the bottom of the ninth inning with a leaping catch against the right field bleachers on a drive by Mantle with two runners on.

The 1956 season will go down as "The Year of the Rhubarb." So many disturbances have erupted on major league diamonds that baseball executives are asking, "why?" Never have so many incidents occurred in a season, bean-balls, name calling, and actual exchanges of blows. All of these things indicate that the situation may be getting out of hand.

If allowed to continue, these bitter rhubarbs could lead to a riot, serious injury to a player or even the forfeiture of a game.

One such rhubarb in Milwaukee will go down in history as one of the more interesting in the game.

Joe Adcock, the Braves' muscular first baseman, literally chased pitcher Ruben Gomez of the Giants off the field at County Stadium, on July 17. The trouble started when Adcock, the Braves' leadoff hitter in the second inning, was hit on the right wrist by Gomez' first pitch. Adcock, who has been injured by pitched balls three times in the last two seasons, yelled something at Gomez and the Puerto Rican yelled back.

Just as Adcock got opposite the pitcher's mound, he swung around and lunged at Gomez. Gomez seemed to freeze for a moment then threw the ball at Adcock, who by that time was only about 15 feet away. Adcock was hit flush on the left thigh.

In a flash, the diamond was covered with players from both teams. After throwing the ball at the 225 pound Adcock, the 170 pound Gomez starting running full tilt and he did not stop until he reached the safety of the visitors' clubhouse. Players tried to tackle the fleeing Gomez, but succeeded in only slowing him down momentarily.

Adcock, in hot pursuit went into the dugout and tried to chase Gomez up the runway, but a host of Giants restrained him. Several policemen arrived to help the four umpires break up the party.

Not a punch was struck, and nobody except Gomez and Adcock seemed angry. Giant players, in fact, offered little sympathy for their teammate.

One Giant said, "He never should have run. What could have happened if he had stood his ground? Maybe one poke and then we would have stopped it." Another remarked, "He'll never hear the last of this, every club in the league will be after him now."

Giants' manager Bill Rigney said, "I wish he had stayed out

there. We would have been out there in plenty of time to save him." Rigney added that he will continue to pitch Gomez against the Braves, "I can't hide him."

Gomez defended his runaway act by saying. "I turned around and saw him charging at me. I deedn't want to get my reebs broke, so I run."

Adcock said, "He called me a name and I chased him. I was never so mad in my life. It's a good thing I didn't catch him."

Within an hour, five plainclothes men escorted Gomez to his room at the Schroeder Hotel. Four uniformed officers stood outside the Giants' clubhouse until long after the game was over.

After the affair, NL president Warren Giles suspended Gomez for three days and fined him $250. Adcock was fined $100. (Bob Wolf)

For any of the 12,084 fans who showed up a week later at the Polo Grounds the night of July 24 expecting a renewal of the Reuben Gomez-Joe Adcock fireworks, the evening was a great big dud. Adcock, who had chased the New Yorker off the mound and into the dugout in as bizarre a footrace as baseball has ever seen, didn't growl at his opponent even once.

Reuben got on base in the second inning through a single and first baseman Joe had some pleasant words for him. "I said, 'How are you Reuben?'" revealed Adcock. "And he said, 'Okay.'"

"Guess if I hadn't lost my head last week, I wouldn't have chased him. But let's forget it." (Lou Miller)

Duke Snider, who allegedly plays baseball for money, not for fun, may not soon forget about a 200 pound electrician from Cincinnati!

But, Ralph Baumel, the electrician probably will never forget The Duke, especially when he fingers his two front teeth he had to have installed after asking Snider a question?

"What's the matter, Duke, ain't you got no guts?" Baumel is reported to have asked as he encountered Snider leaving the field after the Redlegs had pulled out a ninth-inning 4-3 win over the Dodgers.

"I'll show you who's got guts," replied Snider.

Roundhouse swings were exchanged, with the result that The Duke had a mark on his upper lip and Baumel, lost two front teeth from a Snider blow.

The Duke immediately applied for an assault warrant against Baumel. After being taken to the local police station, Baumel countered with a warrant against The Duke, which brought the cops to the Dodgers' hotel somewhere around 3:00 a. m.

At nine o'clock the next morning, The Duke and Baumel appeared in police court before a judge who promptly assumed the role of peacemaker. The judge asked both men to "forget it all."

"I lost two teeth," protested Baumel, pointing to his mouth.

"I'm no dentist," retorted the judge. "You will have to settle the issue of damage to your teeth in a civil court."

As the two stood in front of the judge, Baumel couldn't resist another jab at Snider as they shook hands, "I hope you lose the next two games of this series," he said.

That ended the exchange, and after he returned to the hotel Snider was more philosophical than bitter. "Heck," he said. "The guy called me gutless, or something like that, what am I supposed to do?" (Roscoe McGowen)

Trailing 8-5 going into the bottom of the ninth at Pittsburgh on July 25, the Pirates rallied to defeat the Cubs 9-8 on the first inside the park grand-slam in major league history by Roberto Clemente.

Clemente hit the first pitch thrown by reliever Jim Brosnan to left-center field and raced around the bases behind three teammates for the victory.

Dale Long set a new Pittsburgh record for most homers by

a left-handed batter, with his twentieth of the season in the fourth inning.

July 25 was a good day for walk off homers, as Duke Snider smashed a 400 foot drive over the centerfield fence in the bottom of the ninth against the Redlegs in Jersey City for a 2-1 Dodger victory.

Don Newcombe pulled even with Brooks Lawrence for most NL wins with 14, as he scattered five hits and struck out nine. Lawrence, who allowed only four hits for the Redlegs, lost for the second consecutive time, as his record fell to 14-2. All the runs in the contest were on homers. Frank Robinson homered for the Redlegs and Carl Furillo, hitting safely in his eighteenth consecutive game, homered for the Bums.

This is Phil Rizzuto's last season as a player. The Scooter, who will be 38 in September, made that quite plain as the Bombers left New York for Chicago. Rizzuto indicated that he was open to offers to manage in the major leagues. If the Giants or Dodgers, or some club in the American League, are interested, they will find him in a very receptive mood. He has at least one offer to broadcast games for an unnamed major league team.

"My next move has to be one for happiness," Rizzuto said. "Don't misunderstand me. I am just about the happiest ball player with regard to home and family. But I don't get to see my wife and children enough. It has been a wonderful career, a great source of friendships. Now, who needs a manager?"

Casey Stengel celebrated his birthday, July 29, one day early, in Kansas City. How old is Casey? The book says 65, but that may be a slight error. There are historians who say Stengel lost track of three or four years, but no matter. Happy birthday, Perfesser!

After the Dodgers had played and lost their exhibition game against the Indians in Cleveland, July 23, the traveling secretary, Lee Scott, took the players to a local restaurant to celebrate two birthdays.

Pee Wee Reese had reached his thirty-seventh milestone and Don Drysale, the losing pitcher for the evening had arrived at his twentieth.

The group had a double birthday cake. Pee Wee cut the cake and tried to give the first piece to Roy Campanella as "the oldest player in our set."

That started an argument that went on for hours, with players threatening to produce birth certificates all over the place. Campy insisted that he is three years younger than Reese and Jackie Robinson and five years the junior of Sal Maglie. A good time was had by all!

The Minor Leagues
(Down on the Farm)

Swarms of mosquitoes invaded Capilano Stadium in Vancouver during a July twin-bill between the San Francisco Seals and the Vancouver Mounties. Players in both dugouts built smudge fires to chase the pesky insects. The two teams split the double-header, but players declared the mosquitoes the real winners!

Pacific Coast League umpires have found that the dirt at Vancouver's park is the best anywhere for rubbing up balls, and they take small bags of it after each visit.

A grass fire burned down part of the right field fence at Edmonds Field in Sacramento the afternoon of July 3, necessitating a special ground rule for the Solons game that night.

The next night, Solons coach Ferris Fain was fined $75 and given a five day suspended sentence for starting a fight with San Francisco pitcher Eli Grba in the first game of a double-header. League president, Leslie O'Connor was a spectator at the July 4 event, and also fined Grba $25 and barred both players from the second game.

In the Western League, Dick Stuart raised the sight of his booming bat after he set a modern Western League home run record. The 23 year old Lincoln outfielder said, "I will just keep shooting for the moon and hope the good Lord helps me." Shortly after the half-way point of game number 140 Stuart smashed the record when he hit number 45 at Sioux City. Four nights later, he collected number 46, putting him only 26 behind Joe Bauman's all-time Organized Baseball record of 72 homers in a season, while playing for Roswell in the West-Texas-New Mexico League in 1954.

Stuart, the handsome Pittsburgh farmhand is a movie extra during the off-season. He has appeared as a "dead Nazi" and a "live commando" in the movie "D-Day, 6th of June," and has played several roles in the television production "Badge 714."

"I hope my hitting will take me to the big leagues," he said. "If it does, I know I'll stay there."

In the Sally League, a fifth-inning homer by Harmon Killebrew, until recently a Washington bonus infielder, enabled Charlotte to defeat Columbus, 4-3, before a turnout of 1,738 at the Foxes' park.

In the American Association, Denver hurler, Ralph Terry, a 20 year old right-hander, boosted his record to 8-2 when he weathered a 12-hit attack to beat St. Paul, 11-4.

In Omaha, the crowd was treated to an oddity in the second game of the July 4 double-header when Jim Kite, the Denver starter retired the first eight Omaha batters on high outfield flies. Denver spoiled the holiday festivities as they took both games of the twin-bill from the Cardinals.

Manager Frank Lucchesi of Lake City (Pioneer League) has inaugurated a system of fines to stir up the Bees, including 25 cents for any batter who fails to drive in a runner from third with less than two out. There will also be a fine of 50 cents for any runner who gets picked off base and 50 cents for any pitcher who walks the opposing pitcher. The money will be placed in a player fund to be divided at the end of the season.

Frank Leja, displaying the power that made him the Yankees' first expensive bonus player, tied a Carolina League record when he smashed three homers for Winston-Salem in a 12-7 victory over High Point-Thomasville, on July 4.

A thief sneaked into the Ponca City (Sooner State League) dressing room, stole an estimated $549 from the players' wallets, but fans contributed $286 at the next night's game to help make up part of the losses. Manager Don Biebel split the money among the players on a pro-rata basis.

Luke Sewell, the Seattle Rainiers manager was ejected from the contest against the Hollywood Stars when he came to the aid of his shortstop Leo Righetti who was thumbed from the game for protesting a called third strike. Sewell also drew the heave-ho and let himself in for a possible fine when he neatly piled a stack of dirt on the plate in protest.

Manager Max Macon "kicked" himself out of a game, and there was speculation his parting boot might cost him a fine or suspension. Ejected during an argument, the St. Paul Saints manager tried to kick dust at the home plate umpire, he missed the dirt and kicked umpire Walt Doyle in the shins.

The National Federation of State High School Athletic Officials has appealed to Negro professional and semi-professional leagues to halt the signing of high school youth until they have graduated. Federation executives of the organization said the agreement with Organized Baseball, prohibiting the signing of youngsters before they graduate is working out very well. However, a major problem is developing among several leagues not affiliated with Organized Baseball.

"Let's allow these youngsters to finish school," said H.V. Porter, executive secretary of the organization, "their education is more important than a few dollars and an opportunity to make it to the major leagues is a long shot."

Johnny Podres, former Dodger hurler and 1955 World Series MVP, now in the Navy at Norfolk, Virginia fanned 14 as Norfolk defeated Bainbridge Training Center, 3-1.

Dick Stuart, Organized Ball's home run leader, added a grand slam flourish to his new all-time Western League record when he blasted a powerful four-bagger with the bases loaded in the fifth inning against Albuquerque in Lincoln. It was homer number 50 for the 23 year old Lincoln outfielder, who the inning before had tied the record set back in 1936.

In the Class B Carolina League, back to back homers by Willie McCovey and Leon Wagner after two were out in the eighth inning enabled Danville to cop a 5-4 decision from Fayetteville. It was Wagner's thirtieth four-bagger of the season.

Thieves are all around! About $5,000 in cash and jewelry were stolen from two locker rooms of Carolina League clubs within a 30 minutes period, July 23.

While the Greensboro Patriots were on the field against Wilson in Greensboro, their valuables bag, containing about $2,000 in cash watches and rings, was stolen from the locker room.

Thirty minutes later, at Thomasville, N.C., where the Hi-Toms were playing Durham, an estimated $3,000 in cash and jewelry was taken from the home club's locker room.

Authorities believe the burglaries were committed by the same person, pointing out that the distance between Greensboro and Thomasville can be driven in less than 30 minutes. (Smith Barrier)

Dick Stuart, the Western League's new all-time home run king is a man of his word. On the final night of her visit here in Lincoln, Nebraska, before returning to their home in California with their young daughter, Stuart promised his wife he would hit a home run for her as a going away present.

So he did! He connected in the third inning, again in the seventh inning and again in the eighth, each time with a man on base to help the Chiefs to a 9-8 win. The four baggers were number 52, 53 and 54 for the Pittsburgh farmhand, leaving him only 18 short of the all-time organized ball record of 72. (Don Bryant)

CHAPTER FIVE

Ted "Spits," while Mickey "Hits"
(Standings as of August 1, 1956)

American League				National League			
Team	**W**	**L**	**GB**	**Team**	**W**	**L**	**GB**
New York	67	32	---	Milwaukee	57	36	---
Cleveland	58	39	8	Cincinnati	58	41	2
Boston	54	44	12 ½	Brooklyn	56	41	3
Chicago	48	46	16 ½	St. Louis	48	47	10
Baltimore	45	54	22	Philadelphia	46	52	13 ½
Detroit	45	54	22	Pittsburgh	43	54	16
Washington	40	60	27 ½	Chicago	41	55	17 ½
Kansas City	35	63	31 ½	New York	35	58	22

Hank Greenberg, general manager of the Indians, has taken a rap at what he calls, "a lack of imagination" in planning the American League schedule. Greenberg made it clear that he was especially unhappy about the situation which developed earlier in the season when the Indians had to play 14 games in 12 days against the Yankees and Red Sox.

"I wrote to Mr. Harridge (league president) that I felt this was too much of a penalty to place on one team," said Greenberg. "I also stated that a schedule of that sort has an adverse effect for the entire league. Fans want variety and baseball owes it to the fans to have variety in scheduling. When we go down in the standings, we go down in attendance. We should spread out the games played against the better teams. Fans have only so many dollars to spend."

"Bad work by umpires is driving fans from the ball parks," Cardinals general manager, Frank Lane declared. "I'm not an umpire baiter," said Lane. "In fact, I think it is a crime that a veteran umpire is paid less for doing his job than a utility infielder. But we're getting an awful lot of bad work. What's more, one inefficient umpire in a crew of four can spoil an entire game."

Lane, who charged that Frank Secory "ought to pay to get in to see a game" after the ump ejected Ken Boyer from a recent game, said he had received a long letter from Warren Giles, National League president, in connection with his re-marks.

"Secory put out our hottest hitter in the fourth inning of a close game, Lane said. "Some fans, many of whom had driven 300 miles, told me they weren't going to come that far again to see some quick-thumb umpire show off."

In Milwaukee, Fred Haney has the experience and now he has the "horses," as he is being hailed as a big factor in the Braves surge to the top of the National League. The Braves have shown new spirit and hustle under Haney and the crowds continue to bulge at Milwaukee County Stadium.

Previously, Haney had "tail-ender" teams, heading up the hapless St. Louis Browns and then saw his Pirates managerial time as a consistent cellar dweller, during the Pirates youth movement years.

Haney shrugs off all the miracle man talk. He insists that the players deserve the credit, not him. "If you've got the horses," he says, "you can win. If you haven't, you can't. It's as simple as that."

Hitters like, Hank Aaron, Eddie Mathews, Joe Adcock, Bill

Bruton, Del Crandal and others are driving the Braves. Lew Burdette, Johnny Antonelli, Bob Buhl, Ray Crone and Warren Spahn lead a formidable pitching staff that has the Braves in first place.

Joe Adcock, set a personal record, on the last day of July, when he socked his twenty-fourth homer of the season in a game with the Dodgers at Jersey City. The best previous round-tripper total for the Milwaukee first baseman was 23, set two years ago. The homer was Adcock's fifteenth of the month, only one short of the NL record of 16 set by Ralph Kiner, then with the Pirates in September of 1949.

Despite a run of bad weather in Milwaukee this season, the Braves attendance was pushed over the million mark when they closed their recent home stand in July. With 28 more playing dates at County Stadium, the Braves could still reach the 2,000,000 figure in attendance. They drew two million last year after breaking the league record with 2,131,388 in 1954.

A party of over one hundred Braves' fans accompanied the Milwaukee club on its swing through the East, cheering their favorites vocally and with cowbells, in addition to attending television shows, staging parties and visiting night clubs.

For $180 dollars, a fan received transportation from Milwaukee to New York, Philadelphia, Brooklyn and Pittsburgh, tickets to the games, most meals and sightseeing tours.

"There are no fans like our fans," declared Jim Bird, president of the Braves Booster Club, which sponsored the ten day trip.

On days or nights when the weather is bad, the Milwaukee ground crew takes pride in their ability to cover the field. The crew is so swift with covering the field during showers that one of their crew members tripped and was buried ten yards back before they discovered him and extricated him.

Enos Slaughter believes his is the first big leaguer to have worn a protective helmet. He experimented with one during spring training way back in 1939, although he did not wear one in a game until he returned from the military service. "And thank God," he added, knocking on the wooden bench, "I've never been hit in the head."

Elston Howard, the fine catcher of the New York Yankees says he was so nervous the first time he went behind the plate in a major league game that he called for a pitchout with no one on base.

Ted Williams says he can't understand why he gets booed, he, a great hitter with a .350 batting average. It's not your .350 batting average they boo, Ted. It's your .150 personality! Fans in Boston, and the writers, can get as unpleasant as you can. Don't try to change, though. As a nice guy, you'd be terribly dull. (Dick Young)

Williams' recent homer that enabled the Red Sox to defeat the A's 5- 3 in ten innings was considered by Boston writers to be perhaps the hardest hit by the Splendid Splinter during his major league career. The ball at no time rose higher than 12 feet, yet skimmed over the center field fence 425 feet from home plate. The clout was hit off Bobby Shantz, the A's outstanding lefthander.

Among the gifts received through the mail recently by Williams was a silver spittoon engraved by a New England fan. Asked what he would do with the shiny object, the Red Sox slugger, who had expectorated in the direction of the Boston press box as a sign of contempt for the scribes, replied: "I'm definitely going to keep this among my souvenirs."

Expansion is a topic that has always been heard in baseball circles. Recently, Hank Greenberg made a proposal that baseball look into the possibility of inter-league play. One writer proposed that expansion of each league to nine clubs each, with the two odd teams playing the inter-league game, would be best. An intriguing idea, that eventually took almost sixty years to come to fruition.

Following a defeat by the Yankees in the recent White Sox

series, Manager Marty Marion of the Comiskey's just shook his head and muttered.

"I'd just like to have those extra men ole' Casey Stengel has sitting around him on the bench over there. If we could get those guys we'd fit them in here and there and have ourselves quite a ball club."

"By the way, when you go into the Yankee dressing room, ask Casey about his Denver lineup."

Stengel, who was toweling himself following his shower, chuckled when Marion's message was relayed to him.

"Yeah, I gave Marty the business when we were at the plate before the game exchanging lineup cards," laughed Casey. "I shuffled those cards around and said I had one from Denver and another one from Birmingham and I hoped I wouldn't get them mixed up."

Denver and Birmingham are both Yankee farm clubs reportedly loaded with the finest young talent in all of the minor leagues.

Another record was achieved by Ted Williams, the slugging Red Sox outfielder, when he was slapped with a fine of $5,000 for spitting in the direction of some 30,000 Fenway Park fans on August 7.

While it had been a long time coming, Red Sox General Manager Joe Cronin finally had his way. For years the GM had been in favor of disciplining Ted, but until the August 7 incident, Owner Tom Yawkey had always restrained him.

The Williams fine, which Cronin announced, was for "spitting." He levied it on the left fielder for unbecoming conduct on the playing field. "We cannot condone such action," said Cronin.

"I called Ted at his residence," Cronin declared, "and notified him of the fine. Ted told me he was sorry about his actions. 'The minute I spit,' Ted told me, 'I knew it was the wrong thing to do. I'm sorry I did it. I don't know why I did it?'"

There was no question of the feeling among the Red Sox brass that Ted should be punished for his spitting, the third incident of its kind in Fenway Park within the past three weeks.

Here's how the rumpus came about, leading to the fine that matched the assessment slapped on Babe Ruth by Manager Miller Huggins for breaking training rules in St. Louis back in 1925.

In the top of the eleventh inning of the Red Sox 1-0 win over the Yankees, Williams had dropped a Mickey Mantle fly ball for a two base error. The fans were still booing when Ted made a nice catch of Yogi Berra's fly ball at the fence to retire the side.

As he ran in toward the dugout, he went into his spitting act about halfway between first base and the Red Sox dugout. As he reached the top of the dugout, he turned in the direction of the press box and let go another shot of saliva.

When he entered the dugout, he grabbed his glove, turned around, waved the glove towards the area between home plate and third base and then spat again!

In Boston's turn at bat, after the bases had been filled, Williams walked on a 3-2 pitch by Tommy Byrne, forcing in the winning run. He threw his bat 40 feet into the air as he proceeded toward first base.

"I was teed off," said Williams about throwing his bat high into the air.

A woman, who has been a Sox rooter for years seated near the dugout, was astounded by the action. "Why is he mad?" she asked after the game. "He didn't lose the game; he drew a walk to win it." (Hy Hurwitz)

The longest batting streak of the season in the majors came to an end, August 8, when Hank Aaron was handcuffed by Herm Wehmeier of the Cardinals in the second game of a double-header.

The Braves' outfielder had hit safely in 25 consecutive games before drawing the collar in four trips. Hank batted

.407 during the streak.

Al Kaline, Detroit outfielder, was officially recognized as 1955 Batting Champion of the American League on August 6, when he received the award at Briggs Stadium. Kaline who batted .340 received the sterling silver bat from the Hillerich & Bradsby Company, manufacturers of the Louisville Slugger bat. Kaline became the youngest ever to win a batting title, accomplishing the feat before his twenty-first birthday.

When Brooklyn played an exhibition game in Cleveland, just before Washington came in to play the Indians, several of the Dodgers left a letter for their old boss, Charlie Dressen. "Dear Napoleon," they wrote, "how are the crab fingers coming?" It must be explained that Dressen often used to have flown up from Vero Beach, Florida, cans of crab fingers, a real delicacy.

This is supposed to be a true story. A Washington fan (there are few of them left) came home very late after a night game and explained to his irate wife that it was an extra-inning game. "Well," she said with complete logic, "why don't they start these extra-inning games an hour earlier?"

There's no question that Ted Williams is a ball player's ball player. The phrase is overworked, but the Boston Red Sox slugger apparently has reached the eminence as dean of hitters, as he is constantly consulted by other players for hitting tips.

Are the spitball pitchers getting away with murder again? There have been numerous complaints by batters in both leagues that there are more pitchers throwing spitters and apparently going undetected than ever before. Whenever an umpire calls for the ball and the pitcher rolls it back, it's almost certain the hurler was throwing an illegal pitch. (Bob Addie)

With Duke Snider smashing three homers, a double and a single, the Dodgers won both ends of a double-header from the Cardinals 7-0 and 5-3, to fatten their record to 13 wins in eighteen games against the Redbirds this season. Sal Maglie who hurled the first game shutout, picked up victory number 100 for his career. Sal "The Barber" won his fifth game for the Bums since returning to the National League from Cleveland.

Young Sandy Koufax's trouble continued as the lefty was unable to get out of the second inning in the nightcap due to a lack of control. The fire balling lefty constantly gets behind in the count and then has to throw a fastball down the middle, when major league hitters know it is coming. The Dodgers continue to give the youngster an opportunity, but he is still a ways away from being a complete major league pitcher. Reliever Ed Roebuck took over for Koufax and hurled eight solid innings as the Dodgers rallied for the sweep.

In the American League, Billy Pierce, the majors' top winner, chalked up his seventeenth victory of the season when the White Sox exploded for 11 runs in the first inning and coasted to a 13-3 triumph over the Orioles in Chicago.

On Sunday, August 5, the Tigers defeated the Yankees 8-5, to sweep the three game series and hand the Stengelmen their sixth consecutive defeat. Mickey Mantle homered for the Yankees, his thirty-seventh, to move him 11 games ahead of Babe Ruth's record pace. Bill Skowron and Yogi Berra also homered for the New Yorkers, while Al Kaline belted his third homer of this series and twenty-first of the year for the hometown Tigers.

The next day, Stengel's gamble to start rookie Ralph Terry paid off for the Yankees, as the visiting Bronx Bombers defeated the Red Sox 4-3. Terry, making his major league debut, pitched a strong five innings before wilting in the sixth, but was credited with the win as Tommy Byrne pitched brilliantly in relief, to help the New Yorkers break their losing streak. Fenway Park saw one of its largest crowds of the season, as there were over 35,000 packed in the park.

The young, Terry had been in only two major league parks

before he made his debut. Once as a kid in Oklahoma, he had visited St. Louis and had seen a game at Sportsman's Park, now Busch Stadium, and then he joined the Yankees at Briggs Stadium in Detroit several days before he made his debut.

A ground ball off the bat of Jackie Robinson bad-hopped over third baseman Kenny Boyer's glove for a two-run eighth-inning single that enabled the Dodgers, climaxing a six-run comeback to draw even with the Cardinals in their August 3 night game at Ebbets Field.

Manager Fred Hutchinson of the Redbirds, furious at the most recent weird-reacting grounders in the home of the Dodgers, dashed into the runway behind the visitor dugout, where the groundskeepers store their tools, and came out lugging a pick and shovel he tossed onto the ground in front of the bench as silent significance of his opinion of the Ebbets Field infield.

Hutch was able to grin about it later, for 41 year-old Walker Cooper drove in the runs that gave the visitors an 11-8 triumph in eleven innings.

The Cardinals then headed for Crosley Field in Cincinnati to tangle with the Redlegs. The visiting clubhouse at Crosley, which has been the scene of several top-blowing episodes by Cardinals, witnessed another such incident, after the Redbirds lost a ten inning 7-6 decision to the Reds. Manager Fred Hutchinson, incensed over the tough-luck defeat, drove his fist into the wall to let off steam, bruising his right hand and lacerating the knuckles on his left hand.

Gil Hodges, gunning for Mel Ott's record of driving in at least 100 runs for eight consecutive seasons, will have to step up his pace in the remainder of the season if he is to realize his goal. The Brooklyn first baseman drove in only 63 runs in the first 102 games.

Willie Mays, the speedy Giant outfielder who pilfered 24 bases in 1955, topped that total late in August, when he swiped a sack against the Phillies for number 25 of the season.

An 'Out-Safe' call set off one of the better rhubarbs of the season on August 7 at the Polo Grounds in New York. National League President Warren Giles showed what he thought of Giant Manager Bill Rigney's mix-up with the umpires. Despite receiving a three day suspension and a $50 fine, Rigney's organization believes he was right. So do apparently most of the 7,648 paying customers who booed the umpires loud and persistently following the incident.

After the call, Rigney described it as the worst he ever had seen. Mayo Smith, the Phillies manager who also was involved, was critical, too.

The mix-up started in the eighth inning of the opening game of a twi-nighter, with New York ahead, 3-2, one out and Richie Ashburn on second base.

When Marv Blaylock singled to center, Rapid Richie decided to try for home. Arriving just as Catcher Wes Westrum was reaching for a high throw from Jackie Brandt, Ashburn barged into Westrum, sending both players sprawling beyond the plate.

As they lay there, Westrum called for the ball, which Hoyt Wilhelm had caught while backing up the play. Hoyt flipped it to him and Westrum, still on the ground, turned and tagged Ashburn as the Philadelphian lunged back toward home plate.

Vic Delmore, rookie umpire behind the plate, had been crouched in position all this time, apparently waiting either for Richie to touch the plate or be tagged.

As Westrum tagged the runner, Delmore yelled, "Out!"

That brought Smith and the rest of the Phils erupting out of the dugout, Mayo did an enraged war dance and Willie Jones, his third baseman, had to be restrained from getting closer to the man in blue.

After several moments of this, the umpires succeeded in calming everybody temporarily as they, themselves, gathered for consultation a few yards from the waiting Philadelphians.

In addition to Delmore, they were Jocko Conlan, first base

umpire, and Bill Jackowski, official in charge of third. Missing from this team of play callers was Art Gore, still out with a broken toe suffered at Ebbets Field.

Finally, the three umpires were ready to rule again, "Safe," they decreed.

That sent the happy Quaker debaters back to their enclosure. But now it was the Giants' turn to spring out and scream.

Rigney and Westrum were among the New Yorkers most prominently stomping, gesturing and kicking the dirt. Now both of them had to be restrained from taking violent measures.

Finally, Rigney took off his cap, drop-kicked it high in the air, and tried to charge toward umpire Jackowski. He then was thumbed out and the game resumed.

Stan Lopata, lost no time singling across Blaylock, who in the confusion had taken second. That was the deciding run.

The Giants also lost the second game. But the reverse decision was the one they all were talking about at evening's end.

"Why did Delamore have to ask Jackowski to help him?" demanded Rigney. "Delmore was right on the play, Jackowski was over 100 feet away. How could he see better than the man at the plate? Jackowski is the same guy who was behind the plate on our first trip to St. Louis when Don Blasingame swung at a third strike and Jackowski called it a ball. That umpire has cost us at least four decisions."

Between games, Jackowski had told reporters standing outside the umps' dressing room: "I didn't make the decision. When I was asked, I just told what I had seen. Now, don't crucify me."

Conlan then added: "The runner was safe because of obstruction by the catcher. We didn't call it when he was reaching for the ball and was hit by the runner. But even though it wasn't intentional, he was obstructing when the runner tried to come back and touch the plate."

Jocko then showed the writers Rule 7:04 as it appears in the umpires' manual: "The catcher, without the ball in his possession, has no right to block the pathway of the runner attempting to score. The baseline belongs to the runner and the catcher should be there only when he is fielding a ball or when he already has the ball in his hand." (Lou Miller)

Yogi Berra, Yankee catcher recently told a reporter that he would play every day after he recovered from an injury, added: "Of course, I'll play till I rehurt myself."

Berra's childhood friend, Joe Garagiola commented on his friendship with Yogi, "I never became a strategist because when we were kids Yogi did all the thinking for our team."

A name-calling incident in the recent first-place series between the Braves and Dodgers revived an old feud between Lew Burdette and Jackie Robinson. Robinson, veteran infielder of the Dodgers, issued a challenge to the Braves' pitcher after being angered by what he termed "off-color" remarks by Burdette from the dugout. However, Burdette immediately denied having received an invitation to battle from the Dodger infielder.

As far as could be determined, Burdette called Robinson something like, "watermelon head." It was assumed that the pitcher referred to Robinson's girth, which had been given prominent display in a photograph which appeared recently in a national sport weekly.

Robinson recounted the incident thusly:

"I was tossing the ball to (Gil) Hodges, like we always do before an inning, and I heard Burdette say something about watermelons. I picked up the grounder and threw it to Hodges, and then I listened in case he said anything else.

"He kept saying things that were uncalled for. He wasn't just riding me, I could tell that. Just to make sure, though, I asked Gil whether Burdette meant me. Gil said, "You're number 42, aren't you?"

"The next time Gil threw me a warmup grounder, I heaved

it past him and into the dugout. If the ball hadn't faded, it would've caught Burdette right in the forehead."

Robinson added that he had sent word later to Burdette, presumably through one of the latter's teammates, that he would be available outside the Stadium if Burdette chose to meet him after the game. "He didn't show," Robinson said. "He's got no guts!"

Burdette explained that he merely had "kidded Jackie about his size."

"If that's the way he feels about it," the pitcher continued, "I won't agitate him anymore."

Asked about Robinson's reported challenge to a fight, Burdette said, "I didn't even know I was supposed to fight. No seconds came over with an invitation. Besides, why would we gain by fighting? It doesn't take guts to get yourself suspended. Suppose I'd hit him and hurt my hand, or maybe got suspended. We've got a pennant to win, you know."

Robinson and Burdette have been at odds since September of 1952, when they had words in a game at Boston. Their feud has flared up periodically ever since. (Bob Wolf)

Chuck Dressen, the Washington Senators manager was talking about his plans for managing the Senators next year. Usually he doesn't discuss the bright young prospects in his farm system at all. Chuck did say that "in five years they will be measuring the home runs hit by young Harmon Killebrew." It is believed the Nats will give Killebrew a crack at the third base job next year.

Roy Campanella had the unusual distinction of being called out on strikes on a knockdown pitch in a recent Dodgers game with the Phillies.

Bob Miller, the Phillie righthander, had low bridged Campy and as the Dodger backstop regained his feet, he was notified by Umpire Dusty Boggess that he was out.

"Did I tick the ball?" Campy asked.

When the answer was negative, Roy asked, "Did you get

a signal from another ump that I swung?" Again the answer was no.

"You know what he told me?" Roy reported later. "He said he just missed the call, but I was still out. Imagine that, but what could I say?"

Center Fielder Jim Piersall of the Red Sox put on quite a show in protest against the official scorer's decision in a game at Yankee Stadium on August 15.

In the second inning Piersall grounded sharply to Shortstop Jerry Coleman in the hole. Coleman bobbled the ball twice and the official scorer called an error.

On his arrival at first base, Piersall threw his cap high into the air. Later in center field, he stomped all over, ripping the turf. Piersall remained in a rage until, in the sixth inning he hit a homer. Then he replaced all the divots.

It was the most pronounced demonstration of a player against a scorer's call in recent years at Yankee Stadium. (Dan Daniel)

Manager Bill Rigney of the lowly, New York Giants, who has the ability to muster an occasional smile while trying to dig his way out of the cellar, tells of a letter of encouragement he received the other day from his brother-in-law in California. "When I was feeling very blue," wrote the relative, "I thought of the advice a friend had given me. He told me to forget my troubles, and cheer up; that things could be worse. So, I did what he suggested. I forgot my troubles, and cheered up, and sure enough, things got worse."

While Mickey Mantle attempts to break Babe Ruth's record of 60 homers in a season, one of the most interested observers is Mrs. Ruth, an almost daily visitor to Yankee Stadium when the Bombers are at home. When the Commerce Comet clouted his forty-second round-tripper, August 14, to go 13 games ahead of the Bambino in his record-setting pace of 1927, Mrs. Ruth stood and cheered as Mickey circled the bases.

Although Don Newcombe's scoreless streak was snapped at 39 innings, the Dodger right-hander chalked up his eighteenth win of the season and ninth in a row when he defeated the Phillies 5-2 in Brooklyn on August 14. Big Newk held the Quaker City boys hitless until the seventh inning. Duke Snider and Randy Jackson each homered for the Dodgers in support of Newk.

There will be plenty of high flying ball clubs in the major leagues next season, in the air at least, if not in the pennant races. For years, major league clubs mostly all traveled by rail, but increasing air travel is imminent. Soon, every team will be traveling by air.

Because it is less expensive, because the vast majority of players prefer it, and because they get more time for relaxation and sleep, there is a definite trend toward more plane travel.

Many of the traveling secretaries in the major leagues, who have friends on every main street in America, hate the idea of leaving the railroads, but it is a concession to progress.

"You never forget those long, pleasant evenings and those hours of relaxation in the diners and club cars," said Eddie Brannick, the Giants secretary. "We made a lot of friends that way. I guess many a fellow became a lifelong fan of some ball club because he met the players on a train and got to know them personally. But for a lot of reasons it is better for us now to go by plane.

There are a few major leaguers that are reluctant to fly, but not enough of them to persuade a team to continue rail travel.

Most players do indeed want to fly. "They are in a great hurry to get to the next town and sit around and do nothing, once they get there," said Bill McCorry of the Yankees. "It is like the hare and the tortoise. But that is the way life is becoming in America. You drive down the highway and some fellow goes past you going about 90 and in a little while you go past some roadhouse and he's inside sitting around drinking and doing nothing to be in a hurry about."

The Yankees moved to eight and one-half games ahead of the second place Indians on August 12, as they captured a double-header from the Orioles in New York by the scores of 6-2 and 4-2. Mickey Mantle hit his forty-first homer of the season in the first inning of the opener, to move 13 games ahead of Babe Ruth's record pace. The Mick had three RBI's, while Yogi Berra contributed two solid base hits. The lead over the Indians marked the largest margin at that stage of the race since the 1947 season.

Don Larsen picked up his seventh win of the season in the opener, with a route going performance, allowing only six hits.

In the nightcap, the Yankees rapped Oriole pitcher Bill Wight for a pair of runs in the third inning, highlighted by a two-run triple by Berra. Mantle singled in the fourth and in a display of flashy base-running, scored from first on a single by Hank Bauer.

Two nights later, showcasing their stuff before 52,409 fans, the largest single 1956 night game turnout in the major leagues, Mantle hit his forty-second homer, to stay 13 games ahead of Ruth's pace, and had a perfect night at the plate with two singles and a walk as the Yankees overwhelmed the Red Sox 12-2.

This was Ted Williams' first appearance at Yankee Stadium since his $5,000 spitting fine, and the Splendid Splinter's appearance helped attract the big turnout. Williams could not match Mantle at the plate, as he had only a single in three at-bats.

Indians sensation, Herb Score was doing his best to help the Tribe keep pace, as he struck out 14 Kansas City Athletics in a complete game performance at Kansas City. The flame-throwing lefty moved his record to 12-7.

In the National League, the Redlegs defeated the Braves

8-1 in Milwaukee, enabling the Rhinelanders to move into second place ahead of the Dodgers.

Ex-Giant ace, Larry Jansen, making his initial start following his acquisition from Seattle of the PCL went the distance, allowing nine hits, but did not walk a batter. Redlegs catcher Ed Bailey led the attack as he hit his first career grand slam homer in the eighth inning.

The tightness of the red-hot NL pennant race continued just three nights later, as Eddie Mathews and Joe Adcock homered and drove in three runs each, leading the Braves over the Reds by the score of 6-3, dropping the visitors back into third place behind the Dodgers. Mathews' homer was his twenty-fifth of the season, while Adcock's was his twenty-eighth.

The game was played before 45,003 fans, the fourth largest in the history of County Stadium. Warren Spahn picked up win number 12 of the season and number 195 of his career, as he raised his career record against Cincinnati to 37-13.

Early Wynn passed the 1,400 strike-out mark when he fanned four Tigers at Cleveland, August 14. The Indian right-hander is the fourth active pitcher to pass that mark. Teammate Bob Feller is the leader with 2,573, Warren Spahn of the Braves is second at 1,490 and Virgil Trucks of the Tigers ranks third with 1,431.

Wynn hurled seven innings and left with the score tied at 3-3, but received a no decision, as the Tigers scored three runs in the top of eleventh inning to win by the score of 6-4.

Ted Williams, appearing on Red Barber's "Showcase of Sports," believes Mickey Mantle will break Babe Ruth's home run record this season. "He's got the power, and he has come into his own," said the Red Sox Slugger. "He's in a groove now that great hitters have a way of getting into and he should stay in it for four or five years. With Yogi and Bill Skowron hitting behind him, he has that advantage, too. Their presence means the pitchers have to pitch to Mantle."

Bill Leatherman

The Brooklyn Dodgers had won six straight contests at Jersey City when they ran into the Giants combination of pitcher Johnny Antonelli and slugger Willie Mays. Antonelli hurled a brilliant two-hitter, fanning 11 Dodgers and gained the triumph over Don Newcomb in a 1-0 pitching duel. This was the final game of the season at Roosevelt Stadium, and drew a crowd of 26,385. The Giants victory snapped a nine game winning streak for Newk, and his string of six complete games went down the drain when he was lifted for a pinch-hitter in the eighth inning. Mays' homer in the fourth inning was his second consecutive decisive blow against the Brooklyn club, whom he also beat with a round-tripper the previous night in Ebbets Field.

Frankie Frisch, who suffered a heart attack, August 8, was well on the road to recovery however, his physician announced that he would have to remain in the hospital for three to five weeks. The Hall of Famer, now 57 years old is listed as in 'good condition and no longer taking oxygen.'

It was just a few weeks earlier, on July 4, at the Polo Grounds, when as a sixteen year old fan, this writer obtained an autograph on the back of my ticket stub from Hall of Famer Frankie Frisch, known as the "Fordham Flash."

The Kansas City Athletics gained the dubious distinction of being the first team to be mathematically eliminated from the pennant race when they dropped a double-header to the Indians on August 19, raising their total number of losses to seventy-eight.

The Indians are planning to make Bob Feller Day, in honor of his twentieth year with the club a major event. There will be thirty thousand picture books handed out to the fans on Sunday, September 9, at which he will be honored. These books will contain box scores of Bob's three no-hitters as well as other memorable games during his fabulous career.

For the first time this season, Willie Mays went on a homer splurge, with five in five successive games. He was stopped by Bob Friend of the Pirates, August 18 when it seemed he might have a chance to surpass the record eight straight by Friend's teammate, Dale Long. Earlier in the season, Friend had retired Mays three times on two different occasions.

Bob Lemon of the Indians and Warren Spahn of the Braves moved within three games of membership in the 200 Victory Club on August 19, when they each notched major league career win number 197. Spahn turned back the Reds, 3-1, for his fourteenth victory of the season and Lemon stopped the Athletics 5-2, for his sixteenth triumph.

For the first time in his career, Minnie Minoso wore a batting helmet in the White Sox game with the Tigers, August 18. The outfielder abandoned his previous stand against the protective device as the result of several tight pitches from Virgil Trucks the previous night.

Birdie Tebbetts didn't accuse Lew Burdette of throwing a spitball at Cincinnati, August 20. He just said that the Braves' pitcher violated every rule in the book.

"There isn't a pitching rule he doesn't break," Tebbetts said. "He spits on the ball, he spits on his glove, he spits on his hand, rubs the ball on his uniform. Every one of these things is in direct violation of Rule 8.02"

Tebbetts explained he complained to the umpires several times during the August 20 game. "But they claim," Birdie said heatedly, "that as long as he goes to the resin bag, after doing all these things, then he is absolved of his sins and the resin bag becomes his father confessor."

"I don't think Lew throws a spitter," Tebbetts continued. "He's too high-minded an athlete for that. But I'll say this: If he's not throwing it, then he's missing a heck of a chance."

Informed of Tebbetts' charges, Burdette smiled smugly and said, "Why, I think Birdie was trying to get my goat. He majored in psychology you know!" (Bob Wolfe)

No longer around the National League do they talk with tongue in cheek about Lew Burdette's alleged spitball pitching. Both Tebbetts of the Reds and Bobby Bragan of the Pirates have sounded off on this particular issue.

And now the Phillies' boss, Mayo Smith takes up the issue, saying:

"There isn't any question in my mind, Lew does throw a spitter. This is my own opinion after watching him real close for two years now."

"Burdette loads up five or six pitches every game he works. He's pretty cute doing it, and he's also pretty smart picking his spots. He'll always go for his spitter on a decisive pitch. Generally when he's got a good hitter 3 and 2, or 2 and 2 and he needs a big out to get out of a jam."

"Lew always goes to his mouth to wet the first two fingers on his throwing hand, and then rubs his thumb against his shirt while retaining the moisture on the dampened fingers. This is part of his cover-up, but he isn't fooling me – and a lot of other managers around the league. If we can detect such wrong doing, it's a mystery to me why the umpires can't." (James Enright)

Nellie Fox broke loose on a batting rampage on August 23, rapping seven consecutive hits, to lead the White Sox to a sweep of a double-header with the Yankees, 8-3 and 6-4. The hitting of Fox overshadowed a slump-breaking homer by Mickey Mantle, who belted his forty-third of the season in the nightcap to end a string of nine straight games in which he failed to homer. He is now only five games ahead of Babe Ruth's pace for sixty. Fox was seven for ten on the day as 27,971 fans at Yankee Stadium watched the Bombers fall.

Although not sharp, Don Newcombe posted his twentieth victory of the season at Cincinnati, becoming the first pitcher in either league to reach the charmed circle, when the Dodgers defeated the Reds, 6-5. The Reds hit three homers off Big Newk, to bring their season total to 183, breaking the club record of 181, set last season. Frank Robinson, Wally Post and Ed Bailey each had a round tripper. Newcombe moved his record to 20-6.

It was Saturday afternoon, August 25, at 4:30 o'clock. It was Old Timers' Day in Yankee Stadium, a day of apprecia-tion of what the old players had done for baseball. The pre-game festivities had ended and the Yankees were taking a 4-2 beating from the White Sox.

All of a sudden, a startling announcement was made in the press box. Phil Rizzuto, who had been with the club since 1941, once Mr. Shortstop, who had done so much to win nine pennants in past years, had been released unconditionally.

Rizzuto was stunned. He was sunning himself in the Yan-kee bull pen when he got the news. He went to the clubhouse, dressed, got out his belongings and went home.

Casey Stengel had demanded another outfielder, left hand-ed batter preferred, and he wanted his man before September 1, so he would be eligible for the World Series.

Later in the day, it developed that Rizzuto had been cut loose because the Yankees had recovered veteran Enos Slaughter from Kansas City. Slaughter had been traded to Kansas City back in May of 1955, and now at age forty, he was back.

Scoffing at the reports of the Yankees using Kansas City as their top farm club, one baseball executive asked, with Slaughter going from Kansas City to New York, "was he re-purchased, or just recalled?"

With three years out in the Navy, Rizzuto spent 13 sea-sons with the Yankees. Phil played in nine World Series and four All-Star games. He appeared in more Series games, 52, than any other man in baseball history, having beaten Frankie Frisch's 50 in 1955.

Phil Rizzuto hit .324 and was named American League MVP in 1950, when he beat out such yeoman competitors as Ted Williams, George Kell, Yogi Berra and Joe DiMaggio. (Dan Daniel)

Phil Rizzuto was done! He was the last of the pre-war

Yankees, the little man who was always there! Of course, the end of his playing career was inevitable. At age thirty-eight his future was behind him, but it was rather ironic that Phil should be cut loose to make room for Enos Slaughter who, at age forty, is deemed to be more valuable to the Yankees in another fight for the AL flag.

Phil was one of the stars who resisted the lure of the Mexican raid on the big leagues a few years earlier. One night in New York over shrimp cocktails and filet mignon, Bernardo Pasquel, the brother of Mexican League leader, Bernardo Pasquel, offered Rizzuto $100,000 for three years to play in the Mexican loop, with $45,000 of it in advance.

The story, of course, got out and Phil's teammates had their fun with him. The phone in his room would ring and an unidentified voice would hiss:

"Go down to the soda fountain and buy a milkshake from the blond waitress with the gold tooth. Pay for it with a two-dollar bill and you'll get $100,001.85 in change and an airplane ticket for Mexico City."

Phil would laugh and go down to the soda fountain, and there would be the waitress with the gold tooth and he'd get a soda and ask: "Have you got the money and the tickets?" and naturally the girl would look at him like he had two heads. "I never considered it," he said. "I'd be giving up too much. I've got seven or eight years ahead of me here, yet." (John P. Carmichael, Chicago News)

Done as a player, but would work in the Yankee broadcasting booth for many more years. Phil was a true Yankee and one of the greatest ever!

The Giants climbed out of the cellar on August 25, for the first time since July 4 with a 6-0 win over the Cubs at Wrigley Field, sweeping the four game series. Steve Ridzik hurled his first career major league shutout and win number four for the season with a seven-hitter. Willie Mays led the attack with two doubles, two RBI's and also stole two bases.

Providing a dramatic finish, Joe Adcock homered with two on and two out in the bottom of the ninth inning to give the Braves a 4-1 win over the Pirates, enabling the league leaders to continue one and one-half games ahead of the runner-up Dodgers.

Lew Burdette, who picked up his seventeenth win was staked to an early 1-0 lead when Eddie Mathews homered in the second inning and appeared to have another shutout to his credit until rain forced a 53 minute delay at the end of the eighth. When play resumed, Dale Long, Roberto Clemente and Dick Groat hit successive singles to tie the score at one apiece.

Every time a Cincinnati Reds player belts a home run during the remainder of the season he will be adding to the club's new record. Until this year, no Cincinnati team ever hit more than 181 four-baggers in one season, a mark that was set last season. With over a month to go yet, this season the record is now at 183 and counting.

Fanning three Red Sox to raise his whiff total to 262, Herb Score of the Indians became the first pitcher in modern history to go over the double-century mark in strikeouts in his first two years in the major leagues. Score struck out 245 in his rookie season (1955) last year.

Mickey Mantle, successor to Joe DiMaggio as center fielder of the Yankees, equaled "Joltin Joe's" best home run total for a single season, August 29, when he blasted number 46 in a 7-6 win over the A's.

President Dwight Eisenhower made two separate requests when he made a surprise appearance at Griffith Stadium.

When Mickey Mantle was summoned to the Presidential box before the start of the game, Ike told the Yankee home run king, "I hope you hit a home run, but I hope Washington wins."

Mickey fulfilled the President's request, smashing a home run, number 47 in the seventh inning, but the Senators lost,

6-4, despite three home runs by the Senators' Jim Lemon.

Lemon's first homer, delivered in the second inning with no one aboard, sailed into the regular center field bleachers. His second smash, in the fourth inning after Roy Sievers walked, went into the new seats in left field. His third was stroked into the Yankees' bull pen in left field leading off in the sixth.

After the fame, Secret Service men collared Lemon at Ike's request and escorted Jim to the President for a handshake.

The Minor Leagues
(Down on the Farm)

If any major league club wants to buy Steve Bilko, Los Angeles' hard-hitting first baseman, the "starting price is $200,000" says John Holland, president of the Pacific Coast League club.

Holland added that he wasn't anxious to dispose of Bilko at any price, but was willing to listen to offers in the "$200,000 class." He also said there is no chance of Steve leaving the Angels before the end of the season.

There have been several inquiries from major league clubs on Bilko's availability, Holland said, but he has declined to discuss them at this stage because the Angels have a chance to win the pennant and Bilko is playing a key role.

Through August 1, Bilko had hit 46 home runs and was batting at a .367 clip. The former member of the Cardinals and the Cubs, now owned outright by Los Angeles of the PCL, needs only 14 more circuit blows to tie the Pacific Coast League record of 60 established by the late Tony Lazzeri.

After experimenting with an 11:00 a. m. - 2:15 p. m. starting time for two Sunday double-headers, the San Francisco Seals have made another switch in the Sabbath scheduling. In a move designed to cut down the long wait between games,

Seals officials announced the two remaining Sunday bills on August 12 and 19 would start at 12:00 noon, with the second game booked for 2:15.

In the International League, Satchel Paige continues to sparkle. Satchel leads the league with an 8-3 record and a 1.63 ERA in the 27 games he has appeared for the Miami Marlins.

Paige, the ageless wonder, has become the Marlins' best Sunday pitcher. He has won six of his eight decisions on Sundays. In his Sunday pitching, Paige has worked a total of 37 innings, allowing eight earned runs on 25 hits for a 1.93 ERA. He has scored only two week-day victories in compiling his over-all 8-3 record.

Asked the reason for his remarkable Sabbath success, Paige responded: "I don't know the explanation, unless that it is that I like warm weather and we play most of our Sunday games in the afternoon."

Paige revealed his formula for keeping warm on the cool summer nights in the North-four sweatshirts, a rubber shirt and then his regular baseball shirt. Satchmo, looking bulkier than usual, disclosed he wore that outfit when he struck out Norm Sherry on three pitches to preserve a 6-5 victory in the bottom of the ninth over the Buffalo Bison. "I'm never going to be cold again when I pitch in Buffalo, Toronto and Montreal," declared Satch. (Jimmy Burns)

Satchel was known as one of the nicest and funniest guys that professional baseball has ever seen. He was a comedian and he loved to pull pranks on his teammates. Satch loved gin and vodka, and he would always have a group of his girl friends at the games. They would be dressed to the hilt, carrying their perfume bottles in their dainty purses, but the perfume bottles would be filled with gin or vodka. While he sat in the bullpen area, he would visit with the girls and sip from their perfume bottles, often he would have more than just a sip or two. He would then get a call to come in to pitch and he would usually strike out the side.

The stories abound about the great Satchel Paige. On August 6, 1952 he became the oldest pitcher to throw a complete game, a shutout, when he defeated the Detroit Tigers 1-0 in twelve innings. Satchel was 46 at the time and was pitching for the St. Louis Browns who lost 90 games that season. After his masterful performance in Sportsman's Park he told his manager, Marty Marion that he would not be around for workouts the next day, as he "was going fishing." Satchel Paige had made his major league debut in 1948 with the Browns and was inducted into the Baseball Hall of Fame in 1971.

Luke Easter has stepped up his batting pace considerably since donning glasses several weeks earlier. In his first 22 games while wearing the wide-lensed type of specs, the Bison slugger hit at a .365 clip and hiked his league leading homer total to twenty-three.

International League president Frank Shaughnessy disclosed recently that the suspension he slapped on Havana Sugar Kings Coach Rinaldo Cordeiro for the remainder of the season for was misconduct unbecoming a professional. The basis for the suspension was that Cordeiro allegedly spat on Umpire Frank Guzzetta three times during an argument.

The Charleston Senators of the American Association added a touch of color for a twin-bill recently. When a severe rainstorm hit the park less than four hours before game time, peat moss and sawdust were strewn around the infield to absorb moisture. Since the white foul lines didn't show up well, Groundskeeper George Toma mixed a green dye solution to mark off the foul lines on the tan sawdust. Both Toma and his assistant were knocked to the ground by a bolt of lightning while working during the storm, but both escaped uninjured.

As a gimmick to spur fan interest, the Austin club of the Texas League started an accuracy hurling contest. Each night one fan is given a chance to throw a ball from home plate at a barrel on second base. A prize of $50 was offered the first night, with the award being increased $25 each night until someone throws one in the barrel.

Atlanta Crackers Manager Clyde King has made a practice of picking up the Sunday morning breakfast check for all Crackers who attend church. As a result, at least half of the squad usually shows up for church services.

"Players' Night" at High Point-Thomasville in the Carolina League, drew a crowd of 1,115 fans who contributed about $700 to a fund for members of the club, who lost about $3,000 in a burglary in their clubhouse two weeks earlier. The nights' donation increased the fund to about $1,200.

The famed DiMaggio brothers, Joe, Dominic and Vince never played together as a unit during their organized baseball careers, but the trio was scheduled to come out of retirement and form the outfield for the San Francisco Seals old-timers in an exhibition at Wrigley Field in Los Angeles, August 4, against the Angel old-timers.

Vince stole honors from his more famous brothers before a crowd of 12,158, smashing a homer with a man on base. Joe had a pair of singles. The Los Angeles old-timers won 3-2.

Joe Torre, the 15 year old brother of Frank Torre, Milwaukee first baseman, recently turned in his third no-hitter of the season while pitching for a Brooklyn amateur team.

Ralph Kiner, who gave up his playing career last winter to become Padre General Manager, says his white collar job is driving him nuts or at least to peanuts. "Watching some of these games makes me so nervous I've taken to eating peanuts, and since the start of the season I've put on ten pounds," Kiner declared.

Satchel Paige had three chances to return to the majors this season, but the ageless Negro hurler turned them down in favor of remaining with the Miami Marlins, Bill Veeck revealed while on a visit to Miami last week.

The Marlins' executive vice-president declined to identify the clubs which sought Paige, but it was reported one was the Chicago White Sox and the two others were National League teams.

"My trip here about a month ago was to consult with Paige about his chance to return to the majors," Veeck explained.

"I told Leroy (Paige) it was strictly up to him, and he decided to stick with the Marlins."

Luke Easter hit two of the longest home runs ever seen by Buffalo fans, August 3-5, in hiking his league leading total to 25. The August 3 blast traveled an estimated 480 feet, bouncing along the rooftops of two homes behind the centerfield fence. In the opener of the August 5 double-header, Easter drove a pitch clear over the right field light tower and the ball landed two streets beyond the park, approximately 500 feet from home plate. The drive with two mates aboard enabled the Bison to edge the Cubans 3-2.

Hall of Fame careers have to begin somewhere! The Knoxville Smokies of the South Atlantic League (SALLY) fired their manager, Dick Bartell on August 8 and replaced him with Second Baseman Earl Weaver. His first managerial job offers quite a challenge to Weaver, as the Smokies are in last place, twenty-three games off the pace being set by Jacksonville.

Speaking of knotty problems, what happens when a batter gives a ball a solid whack and the lights go out just about the time the sphere is clearing the infield?

Western League Umpires Gene Haack and Jack Wagner couldn't resort to "I'll rule on it when it happens" because they saw it happen in a Pueblo-Sioux City game on August 5.

Larry Stankey, Pueblo first baseman, was at bat in the ninth inning with two out. After two strikes had been called, Stankey got a good cut on a fastball. The ball had all the earmarks of a homer but while it was still rising the park was thrown into darkness.

There was a 51 minute delay while repairmen worked on the electrical system. When the lights went on and the ball couldn't be found in the playing area, Haack and Wagner were called upon to make a ruling on Stankey's blow. Their verdict: "It was a homer. We knew it as soon as it was hit!"

The Sioux manager protested, but withdrew the protest when his club won, 7-4. (Bill Bryson)

Power-packed Dick Stuart, the hottest prospect in the Pirates' farm system, became the seventh player in the history of Organized Ball to collect 60 home runs in one season when he hit for the circuit, August 4, as his Lincoln club defeated Albuquerque 6-4.

Two days later, the 23 year-old outfielder hit number sixty-one, putting him 11 behind the all-time record of 72 by Joe Bauman of Roswell in 1954.

The first player ever to hit 60 in a season at any level was Babe Ruth in 1927.

In a poll of Carolina League managers conducted by the Winston-Salem Journal, Curt Flood of the High Point-Thomasville club was chosen as the loop's most promising major league prospect. The 18 year-old, recently hit his twenty-second homer of the season. Flood edged Danville First Baseman, Willie McCovey for the honor, capturing five first place votes in the poll.

In Indianapolis, the Indians Roger Maris put on a sprinting exhibition in the bottom of the tenth inning when he hit an inside-the-park home run to win the second game of a double-header with St. Paul, 6-5.

In view of what happened in Miami the night of August 13, Miami fans are inclined to believe Satchel Paige's correct age does not matter.

The week before they had read where Bill Veeck, executive vice-president of the Marlins again argued that Satchel is 56 years old. Paige contends that he is 48.

"They started keeping records on birth certificates in Mobile, Alabama in 1901," Veeck argued. "You won't find Paige's certificate, because he was born before they started keeping records. In 1940, the government required all men up to 38 to register for the draft. Paige didn't register, because he did not come under the age limit."

The reason the fans think all of this is irrelevant is that Paige held the Rochester Red Wings to one hit in the seven-inning opener of a double-header and won, 4 -0. Satchel only gave up a fourth inning single.

The victory was Paige's tenth against three defeats and his second shutout. His earned-run average for over 80 innings of work was a scintillating 1.50. (Jimmy Burns)

The latest chapter in "Great Expectorations of 1956" found umpire Don Pieretti of the Arizona-Mexican League paying a court fine of $150 despite the efforts of the league president, Tim Cusick to come to his defense.

Pieretti was found guilty of "simple battery" by the local Justice of the Peace, on August 29, after a parade of six (fans) witnesses testified the umpire had unleashed a watery barrage against them during a game at Douglas the previous night.

Patrons sitting in their private box stated that Pieretti started spitting toward them in the fifth inning and continued the barrage each inning thereafter.

Pieretti, on the stand in his own defense, said he had been injured by pitched balls during the game and was coughing up blood. As a result, he said he had to expectorate throughout the game. President Cusick, argued that it was improbable that Pieretti had spat without provocation from the stands. "The case is closed as far as the Arizona-Mexican League is concerned," the president added. (Ben Foote)

Following a season-long poll of fans, John Glenn, Negro centerfielder for the Macon Dodgers, was named the most popular player of the Sally League club. It was possibly the first time a Negro player had received such an important baseball honor in the Deep South.

Hank Aaron was voted the Sally's MVP while with Jacksonville in 1953, and Juan Pizarro, a rookie Jacksonville hurler, won the award this season, but they were named by the league's writers. Glenn's selection was by the fans, who were entitled to one vote each time they purchased a score card during the season. Club officials estimated about 90 per cent of the score cards were purchased by white fans in attendance at Macon games. (Sam Glassman)

CHAPTER SIX

Braves, Dodgers, Redlegs
(Standings as of September 1, 1956)

American League				National League			
Team	**W**	**L**	**GB**	**Team**	**W**	**L**	**GB**
New York	83	47	---	Milwaukee	79	49	---
Cleveland	74	53	7 ½	Brooklyn	77	51	2
Chicago	70	57	11 ½	Cincinnati	76	53	3 ½
Boston	69	58	12 ½	St. Louis	63	66	16 ½
Detroit	63	65	19	Philadelphia	60	65	17 ½
Baltimore	57	70	24 ½	Pittsburgh	55	74	24 ½
Washington	53	74	28 ½	Chicago	51	77	28
Kansas City	41	86	40 ½	New York	50	76	28

Interesting to note, the Cincinnati Reds were called the "Redlegs" until late in the 1956 season, when sportswriters and fans alike began to refer to the Rhinelanders as the "Reds." As the first professional baseball club, they were originally called the "Red Stockings."

After reading so many stories about his Braves cracking in their pennant bid, Manager Fred Haney tried a little psychology before a recent game. He installed a record machine in the clubhouse and greeted his players with the hit tune, "You Gotta Have Heart," from the Broadway musical, "Damn Yankees."

With a red-hot three-way National League pennant race destined to go down to the final week or even the final day of the season, preparations are being made in the event of a three-way playoff.

A round-robin tournament will be conducted to determine the winner in the event Milwaukee, Cincinnati and Brooklyn finish in a three-way tie, President Warren Giles announced last week.

Giles offered the following illustration: "The rule states that, in the event of a three-way tie, the league president shall arrange a playoff series to start as soon as is physically possible, to be played on the home grounds of the three clubs. A team would be eliminated after two losses. In other words it's a two-and-out series. The president is directed to draw lots as a result of which of the three clubs would be designated to play at home first, second or third."

"After this point, each club would have played the other two one time and it is possible one of them would be eliminated. If not, if each team had won one and lost one, the series would continue."

All the difficulties in the round robin would work themselves out, but might possibly delay the World Series.

"Certainly, the odds are against three clubs playing 154 games and winding up with exactly the same number of wins and losses," the NL prexy added. "Nevertheless, the Braves, Dodgers and Reds appear to be so evenly matched that it is not beyond the realm of possibility that we might have the first three-way tie in history in 1956."

"At any rate, if all this should happen, we'll be ready for it!"

The tight NL race moved into September with only twenty-five games left in the schedule.

The Dodgers climbed to within two games of the pace

setting Braves when they swept the afternoon-night double-header on September 1 from the Giants 5-3 and 5-0. Don Drysdale gained credit for his fourth victory of the year in the opening game, but needed help from Clem Labine to close it out.

Sal Maglie and Don Bessent combined to hurl a two-hitter in the nightcap as Sal "The Barber" won his eighth game of the year. The contest was the first for Maglie as a foe in the Polo Grounds, but he wasn't around at the finish to enjoy it.

When Umpire Al Gore called a ball on a 3-1 count to Foster Castleman in the sixth inning, Sal blew his top. The normally impassive Maglie squawked and slammed his glove to the ground. Gore immediately waved him out of the game, and the Dodgers, led by Walt Alston and Roy Campanella, did a war dance around the umpire. Gore pointed out that throwing a glove meant an automatic exile.

It was tough on Brooklyn, because Sal had allowed only one scratch hit for five and one-third innings. Calling Bessent in to finish the contest meant that he would not be available the following day, when the Dodgers ultimately would lose two to the lowly Giants.

The Giants handed a devastating double defeat on the Dodgers, by the scores of 2-1 and 4-1, to drop the defending champions into a tie for second place with the Reds, three and one-half games behind the pacesetting Braves. Johnny Antonelli out dueled the Bums Carl Erskine in the opener, with both hurlers completing route going performances.

In the nightcap, the Giants took advantage of wildness by young Sandy Koufax to defeat the Dodgers 4-1. In only four innings of work Koufax allowed five runs on five hits and four bases on balls. Willie Mays and Foster Castleman homered for the Giants, while Jackie Robinson had a solo shot for the Dodgers. Castleman's blast was a three run homer that sealed the victory.

The Giants, working desperately to climb out of the cellar

with the Cubs, were determined to be spoilers for their hated rival Dodgers.

In Milwaukee, sparked by the two-hit pitching of Warren Spahn and a clutch single by Joe Adcock, the Braves defeated the Cardinals 3-1, before 24,745 fans. Spahn was magnificent, as he hurled a two-hitter, one of those a home run by Cardinals outfielder Wally Moon. Hank Aaron homered in the fourth inning to give Spahn a lead the Braves held until Moon tied it at 1-1 in the eighth inning. In the bottom of the eighth the stage was set for Adcock's heroics, as he drilled a two-out single for what proved to be the winning runs.

The Reds kept pace with a 7-3 home field win over the Chicago Cubs, behind a complete game performance from Brooks Lawrence, who grabbed his seventeenth win at Crosley Field.

Just two days later, it was Lawrence working in relief of Larry Jansen, hurling seven innings of outstanding ball to help the Reds earn a split in Milwaukee with the Braves. Lawrence picked up his eighteenth win of the season before the largest crowd of the year in Milwaukee, 47,664.

In the opener, Lew Burdette pitched the hometown Braves to a 3-2 victory, as he scattered 10 Reds hits for his eighteenth win. Hank Aaron gave Burdette all the run support he would need with two home runs. Aaron thrilled the record crowd with another homer in the nightcap, for a three homer day and he also added two doubles.

Birdie Tebbetts' recent charge that Lew Burdette of the Braves is throwing a spitball drew a laugh from Spud Chandler, former Yankee ace and now a scout for the Kansas City A's.

"That's real funny, because ole' Birdie is just getting back some of 'em he used to call for when he caught for Detroit," Chandler told Don Oliver of the Reporter-News.

"Man, when he was behind the plate and Tommy Bridges was on the mound you could always expect that spitter when they got in a jam. Sometimes you could see the spit dropping off that ball in mid-air, but Birdie would grab the ball and wipe it clean before the umpire had a chance to look it over."

Chandler continued, "One time, though, it backfired on Birdie. We were playing them and Joe Gordon was at the plate, Bridges came in there with the spitter and Joe knew what was coming. He reached back and tried to take the ball away from Tebbetts before Birdie could clean it off. You should have seen the wrestling match that took place right there at home plate. That was the funniest thing I ever saw. But, by the time Gordon got the ball, all the evidence had been wiped off." (Don Oliver, Reporter-News)

Willie Mays, who stole his thirty-third base in a game against the Dodgers, September 8, came through with his thirtieth homer of the season against the same Dodgers the next day and thereby became the first player in the 80-year history of the National League to go over the 30-mark in both stolen bases and home runs in the same season.

An American League record for home runs in a season was established on September 12, when home run number 974 was hit in Kansas City by Hank Bauer of the Yankees in a contest won by the Athletics, 7-4. The old record of 973 was set in 1950.

The Brooklyn Dodgers will leave immediately after the World Series, regardless of whether they are participants in the classic, for a 25 game tour of the Pacific in which they will be advertised as "the most exciting team ever to play in Japan."

Twenty games will be played in Japan, three in Hawaii and two in Okinawa.

"The big thing about the Dodgers is that all of the stars are going on the trip," said Solaro Suzuki, the organizer of the Far East trip. "The Japanese people will be delighted to see such stars as Duke Snider, Don Newcombe, Pee Wee Reese and Jackie Robinson."

The tour will begin on October 10, immediately after the World Series is concluded and end on November 17 with the last few days designated for sightseeing in Japan. (Carl Lundquist)

A delegation of fans from Commerce, Oklahoma attended the Yankees-A's game of September 12 but couldn't root Mickey Mantle out of his worst slump of the season. Mickey went hitless, giving him 0-for-12, and had failed to crack a homer or even drive in a run for ten games since he obliged President Eisenhower with number 47 in Washington on August 31.

The chief Yankee gunner entered the month of September two up on Ruth's magic number of 60, but suffered the aforementioned slump, and had only 17 games remaining as the club opened its final western trip.

However, the switch-hitter has an excellent chance to nab the Triple Crown, consisting of homers, average and RBIs. (Joe King)

Max Surkont aims to become an umpire when he's through pitching. "You should make a good one," Sal Maglie said to him. "You certainly are fat enough." Surkont denies he's throwing a spitter now, but readily admits he was loading them up two years ago. "I stopped using it," he adds, "because too many of them were sailing out of the park. If everybody threw a spitter as lousy as I did, the hitters would be yelling for it to be legalized." Max says Preacher Roe gave him lessons on how to get away with it, "but he wouldn't teach it to me until I got traded to Pittsburgh. When I was with the Braves, I asked him to do it, but he refused. He said the Braves could hurt Brooklyn's chances for the pennant. When I got to Pittsburgh, he apparently figured that club couldn't hurt anybody, I guess." (Dick Young)

Dusty Rhodes (of the Giants) and a native of Montgomery, Alabama, cradle of the Confederacy, says; "I may be ridden out of town when I get home, but I've got to say this.

Jackie Robinson is just great. If he doesn't make the Hall of Fame, something is wrong with the guys doing the picking."

On September 8, the skidding Braves suffered their fifth consecutive defeat when they dropped a 3-1 decision to Moe Drabowsky of the Cubs, in Chicago. The young right-hander, allowed only five hits, and fanned five in out-dueling Lew Burdette, who was in search of his nineteenth win of the season.

Meanwhile, the Dodgers moved to within one-half game of the pace setting Braves, with a 4-3 win over the Giants. Willie Mays had three hits, an RBI and a stolen base for the visiting Giants. Don Bessent working in relief of Roger Craig got the win for the Bums. Bessent hurled two scoreless innings, and drove in the deciding run with a sacrifice fly.

Backed by the slugging of Stan Musial and Wally Moon, each with three hits, the Cardinals defeated the Reds, 6-4. Tom Poholsky went the route for the Redbirds. The defeat dropped the Rhinelanders into third place, one-half game behind the second place Dodgers.

In the American League, the Yankees held a commanding eleven game lead over the second place Indians, as the Bronx Bombers exploded for 20 hits, walloping the Senators 16-2, as they moved closer to clinching their second consecutive pennant and seventh in the last eight years. Hank Bauer, the Yankees leadoff hitter had three hits and four RBI, as he socked a homer, triple and a double. Yogi Berra added three hits to the attack, to help Tom Sturdivant earn his fourteenth win.

Dale Long clouted what is believed to be one of the longest home runs ever hit in Forbes Field on September 11, when he connected off the Cubs Bob Rush. The drive into the upper deck in right center field was measured the next day as it came to rest 485 feet from home plate.

Whitey Ford picked his twelfth runner off base this season when he nipped Ted Lepcio of the Red Sox off first base, September 7. Lepcio was the third Boston runner victimized that day by the lefty Ford, who earlier had picked off Billy Goodman and Don Buddin.

Requests for World Series tickets should Cincinnati win the National League pennant have been set..

If the Reds enter the Series, ticket prices, including all taxes will be: Bleachers $2.05, standing room $4.10, reserved seats $7.20 and box seats $10.30. No announcement has yet been made on how and when tickets can be ordered.

The Reds flag hopes received a sharp setback on September 12 when lefty Johnny Antonelli of the Giants hurled a three-hitter, scattering three singles for his eighteenth victory, to defeat the visiting Reds 8-0. The defeat dropped Birdie Tebbetts club to three games behind the pace-setting Braves. Only 1,839 fans showed up in the Polo Grounds, adding more fuel to the fire regarding a possible relocation for the Giants franchise.

Offseason work for major league players is becoming more and more in vogue. Several MLB players have opened bowling alleys, but bowling isn't the only source of additional income for baseball's name-men. Roy Campanella, the Dodger catcher, operates a liquor store in Harlem. Monte Irvin of the Cubs and Don Newcombe of Brooklyn own package stores in New Jersey and actually work in their stores during the off season. Ted Williams of the Red Sox is in the fishing tackle business with Sam Snead in Florida, and Stan Musial, pride of the Cardinals, owns two restaurants in St. Louis and is vice-president of a bank.

Joe Adcock, the Braves' slugging first baseman, owns a cattle farm in Louisiana. Twice he has been wiped out by the drought, but he is back in business. Hank Bauer of the Yankees owns a card in Kansas City's steam-fitters union.

Pitcher Bob Friend of the Pirates is a stock broker all year 'round. Jim Piersall, the Red Sox outfielder works for a chain store system in New England. Gil McDougald, the Yank shortstop, is a designer for a shoe corporation.

At least 12 other major leaguers are known to work at selling automobiles during the off season.

Don Newcombe, the major leagues' winningest pitcher, already has revealed how he'll pitch to Mickey Mantle and Yogi Berra IF the Dodgers get into the World Series.

"I'll pitch high and outside to Mantle," Newk told Jack Lescoulie on the latter's "Meet the Champions" TV show.

"I'll take my chances on cutting the corner for a strike or giving Mickey a ball," Newk said.

"Yogi Berra?" Newk went on. "For Yogi the best bet is to throw it right down the middle, because Berra will swing at and hit almost anything. If I threw it behind his back he'd probably belt it."

Newcombe got into the spitball talk, too, by expressing his firm belief that Lew Burdette, the Braves' ace, and several other pitchers in the National League throw spitters.

"But," added Newk, righteously, "I've never thrown it and don't intend to. I don't need that pitch." (Roscoe McGowen)

Former great Yankee hurler, Spec Shea has dates available for his annual All-Star team to tour the New England area after the current season ends. The tour will open October 11 in New Haven, Connecticut, ending with an exhibition in Pawtucket, Rhode Island. Community leaders can contact Shea's group manager, John Pollidoro, so dates in your area can be scheduled.

The tour gives fans unable to attend major league games the opportunity to see some of MLB's stars perform versus local community stars. It also will generate additional income for those participating MLB players.

Those players already committed to the Spec Shea Tour are; Ted Lepcio, Don Hoak, Moe Drabowsky, Billy Gardner, Walt Dropo, Dale Long, Ike DeLock, Frank Thomas, Art Ditmar, Rocky Colavito, and Sammy White.

Everyone agrees that Cleveland had by far the best pitching staff in the American League this season, with such performers as Early Wynn, Bob Lemon, Herb Score, Mike Garcia, Ray Narleski, Don Mossi and others, but apparently pitching isn't everything. Connie Mack once said pitching was seventy-five percent of the game, but statistics can be deceiving, Cleveland had three 20 game winners in 1951 and '52 and finished second each year with identical records of 93-61.

Now that an inventor has come up with a "speedometer" on bats to test the speed of a swing, we can expect another silly record to go into the books. Bill Skowron is reported to swing the fastest bat at 116 miles an hour, beating even Mickey Mantle, who was clocked at 114 right-handed and 112 left-handed. Has anyone thought of clocking the speed of ball players getting into the diner when they board a train after a long double-header?

Before Warren Spahn of the Braves entered the 200 Victory Club, on September 13, he received the good wishes of Bob Lemon of the Indians, who had won number 200 only two days earlier.

Lemon sent Spahn a telegram which read: "They say the first 199 are the toughest, but it's better to have 200 out of the way. Wish you a lot of luck in your next outing. Good Luck. Go get 'em."

The telegram was signed, "Bob (200) Lemon."

Warren Spahn garnered win number 200 later the same evening after receiving the telegram from Lemon. Number 200 came with a twelve inning 4-3 triumph over the Phillies. "I thought this would be an anti-climax after six 20 game seasons, but it sure isn't. Nothing can compare with winning 200. It's the biggest thrill I've ever had. Also, it meant a lot that my victory contributed to our drive for the pennant. After all, that's what we're really interested in."

Spahn, whose salary now is reported in excess of $40,000 a year, was paid a mere $80 a month when he broke in with the Bradford (Pony League) club back in 1940.

"All I ever wanted to do was play baseball," he recalled. "I was just out of high school and while I wasn't getting much money, I was doing better than some of my friends who started out at $15 a week. Besides, I was doing what I always wanted to do." (Bob Wolf)

The Yankees clinched at least a tie for their twenty-second pennant in club's history by defeating the Indians, 10-3 in the opener of a double-header on September 16. The Bombers wrap-up of the pennant was delayed when they lost the second game of the twin bill 4-3.

Two days later, the Yanks won their seventh pennant in eight years under manager Casey Stengel, and the twenty-second in the club's history when Mantle smashed his fiftieth homer of the season in the eleventh inning for a 3-2 victory over the host White Sox.

Mantle connected off lefty Billy Pierce, who was seeking win number twenty-one. Whitey Ford, who was in search of win number twenty for the Yankees, pitched ten strong innings against the Pale Hose, despite only striking out one batter.

Mantle's homer gave him the distinction of being the only Yankee other than Babe Ruth to hit 50 in one season. However, the young slugger fell eight games behind the Babe's record pace of 60 in 1927.

Quite possibly, the wonderful times connected with Ebbets Field in Brooklyn may soon be coming to an end. There are many peculiarities connected with the Dodgers and their home field.

Ebbets Field undoubtedly is the only park whose press bar was once presided over by a former milkman, who, in addition, pitched batting practice for the Dodgers.

It also is probably the only park in which a woman fan approached a policeman, and, pointing to a National League umpire, said: "Officer, do your duty. Arrest that man, he robbed the Dodgers."

The Flatbush Park is the first major league field at which

Branch Rickey attended a Sunday game. The date was April 25, 1943, and he suspended his practice of refusing to attend games on the Sabbath in order to make a spiel for War Bond sales.

Yes, anything can happen in Ebbets Field!

Gaining revenge for a 6-5 loss in the previous night's game, the Dodgers overwhelmed the Cardinals 17-2, on September 19 to move one-half game ahead of the Braves, who were rained out in Pittsburgh. Don Newcombe, posted his twenty-fifth win of the season and smashed two homers, leaving after seven innings and turning things over to reliever Don Bessent.

Al Dark and Stan Musial each homered for the Cardinals, while Sandy Amoros and Don Demeter homered for the Bums. Duke Snider had four hits and three RBI's.

Meanwhile, in Philadelphia, Curt Simmons and Robin Roberts hurled the Phillies to 4-3 and 7-4 victories in a twi-night doubleheader with the Reds, virtually eliminating the Cincinnati club from the pennant race. Roberts' win was his eighteenth of the season against sixteen losses.

The story of how Mickey Mantle overcame his "shyness" and joined in singing a cowboy song in a Kansas City night club was related by songstress Margaret Whiting in an interview on NBC. Miss Whiting, who described Mickey as "a very shy boy," said the Yankee slugger asked her to sing the song and promised to visit the night club if she would do the number. He not only kept his word, but he also "got up on the floor and sang with me," the vocalist reported. "He was just great."

As the regular season winds down, Major League Baseball has made a significant change for the 1957 season.

The present rule, requiring a batting champion to have at least 400 official times at bat before he can be declared top man will be altered.

Instead, the rule will require a certain number of times for a batter to face a pitcher. The new number will probably be in the range of 550 times, although a lower number may be agreed upon after discussions with statisticians. Changes are needed as some players are often walked more than others and should not be penalized. Walks, sacrifices and hit-by-pitches should count as plate appearances.

The current rule has prevented Ted Williams from winning the batting title in the American League for the past two seasons, and might cost him the crown again this year. Williams last season batted a lusty .356 but Al Kaline of Detroit won the title with a .348 average. Williams was at bat only 320 times officially in 1955, far short of the league figure.

In 1954 the same situation prevailed when he batted .345 but was up officially only 386 times. Bobby Avila of Cleveland won the title with a .341 average.

Thus, the whole idea is to get the rule into proper focus so that no player may be denied the bat title on a fluke. Any batter, who draws frequent walks, is hit often by pitches, or who delivers sacrifice bunts and sacrifice flies, is providing offensive help as valuable as base hits.

Pennant fever was in the air heading into the final days of the National League race. On September 21, a two run homer by the Pirates Frank Thomas in the seventh inning at Pittsburgh enabled the Pirates to defeat the Dodgers by the score of 2-1. Brooklyn's lead over Milwaukee now was only two percentage points, as the Braves defeated the Cubs 6-4.

A loud and boisterous crowd of 30,397 turned out in 55 degree weather to cheer on the Braves and Warren Spahn who earned win number nineteen, although he struggled in the later innings. Leading 6-0 in the eighth inning, Spahn was in need of relief from Gene Conley as the Cubs tallied four runs.

The Cincinnati Reds held on to their faint pennant chances at home as they defeated St. Louis 9-1 behind two homers and a triple by Wally Post.

Baseball experts could not remember when there had been a tighter race, particularly with three teams still in the hunt.

Both the Dodgers and Braves lost on the night of September 22, while the Reds enjoyed a five-run third inning explosion on the way to a 6-4 win over the Cardinals. The Rhinelanders featured homers by Gus Bell and George Crowe to move within two games of the lead.

On Sunday, September 23, the Dodgers who held a lead of 8-3 over the hometown Pirates with two out in the top half of the ninth inning, were forced to surrender first place to the Braves by one percentage point, when the Pennsylvania curfew law prevented the completion of the game. The umpires called time, as required by law at 7:00 p.m. (EDT). The contest was to be resumed the next night preceding the regularly scheduled game.

Playing before 44,932, the largest crowd in history at Forbes Field, the clubs started action in sunlight, but two thunderstorms developed during the afternoon, each causing half of an our delay.

Don Newcombe, in search of victory number twenty-six, pitched the entire distance for the Bums, despite the long waits.

Four homers by the Reds, bringing their club total to 220 for the season, only one under the major league record, powered the Cincinnati club to a double header sweep of the St. Louis Cardinals, 3-2 and 5-4 before 29,840 Reds faithful, hoping for a miracle finish to the season.

Behind a grand slam home run by Bill Bruton, the Braves defeated the Cubs by the score of 7-4 to maintain a percentage point ahead of the Dodgers.

The next day (Monday, September 24), the Dodgers returned to first place with the win in the suspended contest, but were promptly knocked back when they lost the regularly scheduled game to the Bucs by the score of 6-5. The idle Braves regained the league lead by one percentage point.

Bob Friend of the Pirates was the thorn in the side of the Dodgers with his route going performance for his seventeenth win of the season, despite surrendering two homers to Dodger first sacker, Gil Hodges.

On Tuesday, Warren Spahn, the mainstay of the Braves pitching staff, defeated the Reds 7-1 for his twentieth victory of the season and enabled Manager Fred Haney's club to remain one-half game ahead of the Dodgers, who beat the Phillies in a night contest. The Reds defeat dropped them to three and one-half games off the pace for the lead.

The real excitement of the evening belonged to the Dodgers, Sal Maglie! Maglie made 118 pitches as he hurled his first career no-hitter, defeating the Philadelphia Phillies 5-0 in Brooklyn. The 39 year old Maglie was in complete control as he walked two and struck out three. On the two passes he issued he went to a full count on both. He allowed one other baserunner, when he hit Richie Ashburn with a pitch in the ninth with a count of one ball and two strikes on Ashburn.

Sal knew he was working on a no-hitter. "I've been around long enough to know what's going on," he said. "It didn't bother me one bit."

"It wasn't the first time I had a no-hitter going in the late innings. In fact, I believe I did a couple of seven inning jobs on this same club before someone got a hit."

Carl Furillo of the Dodgers, once alleged to be the bitter enemy of Sal Maglie, feels differently now that Sal is on his side.

After Maglie's no-hitter, Furillo had this to say: "That guy should get the most valuable player award on this club. He really has the guts and the ability." (Roscoe McGowen)

After failing to hit a homer at Boston in the first eight games this season, Mickey Mantle connected for a near-record clout in the second inning on September 21. The ball struck the retaining wall in the centerfield bleachers, 487 feet from the plate, and missed by inches of clearing the wall, a feat performed previously only by Jimmie Foxx and Hank Greenberg.

Almost to the man, the Dodgers sounded off against the ball-and-strike decisions by umpire Babe Pinelli after the Dodgers had bowed to the Pirates 6-5 at Forbes Field, September 24.

Jackie Robinson was most vehement of all, declaring, "He called Gil Hodges out before the ball had even left the pitcher's hand. And he missed two on Dale Long in the eighth inning."

The Dodgers contended that Long had fanned on a three-and-two pitch, but Pinelli maintained the batter had halted his swing. The pass to Long paved the way for Frank Thomas to rap the game winning single.

The largest crowd in history for a single game at Milwaukee County Stadium and another record turnout at Forbes Field in Pittsburgh boomed the National League's attendance to 127,920. With no pennant race in the American League to spin the turnstiles, the entire league drew only 53,548 for the day.

On September 26, Robin Roberts of the Phillies handed a severe setback to the Dodgers pennant hopes, as the ace right hander hurled a magnificent 7-3 victory over the pennant hungry Bums. Although yielding only five hits, Roberts set a major league record for allowing the most home runs in a season, including two round-trippers by Duke Snider. The blows brought Roberts' season total of home runs allowed to 43, breaking his own record of 41 set last year. The victory was Roberts' nineteenth of the season, while Don Newcombe took the loss for the Dodgers. Newcombe's record falls to 26-7, as he appears to be the top contender for baseball's first Cy Young Award.

With only three games remaining on the league schedule for each team, the Braves lead the Dodgers by one game. The Reds, while still mathematically alive, must win out, while both the Dodgers and Braves must lose their remaining three games.

In the American League, the Yankees have been on cruise control for most of the second half of the season. With just three games remaining on the slate, the Bombers have a ten game lead on the second place Cleveland Indians.

Lefty Herb Score of the Indians won his twentieth game of the season, joined teammates Bob Lemon and Early Wynn in the charmed circle, when the Tribe defeated the Athletics 8-4 to clinch at least a tie for second place behind the Yankees. The Indians need only one more win or a White Sox defeat to clinch the runner-up spot.

Score posted win number twenty against nine defeats with a nine inning, seven hit performance, striking out 12 Kansas City would be hitters. He boosted his league leading strikeout total to 263. In addition to the trio of Cleveland pitchers with twenty wins, Billy Pierce of the White Sox and Frank Lary of the Tigers each have twenty wins.

Sal (The Barber) Maglie was the guest of honor when the new Remington electric shaver was introduced at a press party in the Hotel Plaza in New York City, September 27 two days after the Dodger right-hander had hurled his no-hitter against the Phillies.

Del Baker, the eagle-eyed first-base coach of the Red Sox was stumped in his effort to steal signs from Don Larsen, because the Yankee hurler worked the entire game without taking a windup. Even when the Bosox had no runners on base, Larsen refused to take a windup, holding the ball at his waist before swinging into the pitch. "It was something new," Baker admitted. "I never saw a pitcher do that through an entire game. I have seen pitchers quick-pitch on a hitter occasionally, but I never saw a man go through an entire game the way Larsen did."

When only 365 fans turned out in threatening weather to see the Indians defeat the Senators in a double-header at

Municipal Stadium in Cleveland on September 19, the Nats' share of the gate was approximately $90.

When was Mickey Mantle actually signed by the Yankees? Where and for how much?

For the benefit of future baseball historians researching the files of The Sporting News, Tom Greenwade (the scout who signed Mantle) has revealed the details.

"I signed Mickey to a Class D contract with Independence, Kansas, while sitting inside my car during a driving rain in Baxter Springs, Kansas, right after a Ban Johnson League game. I told Mickey's father that I thought the boy would be able to play Class D and when he asked how much it would pay, I told him, '$140 a month.'"

"Mickey's father said the boy could make that much playing Sunday games at Spavinaw (Mickey's birthplace) and working around the mines during the week. So I got a pencil and a large manila envelope and we figured out just how much Mickey could possibly make doing a lot of things, and then how much he'd make playing in Class D. It figured up to a difference of $1,150, so that's what I paid him as a bonus. It had to come as a check from the Independence club, naturally, and until that club folded I remembered they had that check framed in the office."

Greenwade also revealed that Mantle had graduated from high school on a Friday, had played a game Friday night and had a game scheduled for Sunday. "I had to get over to see a prospect in Broken Arrow, Oklahoma, and I was mighty scared that some other scouts might get on Mickey's trail while I was away, but Mickey's father promised me that no matter what the offer was, he wouldn't sign until I got back. No scouts showed up and we had Mickey all to ourselves, but I always knew that Mickey's father wouldn't have signed, just like he promised." (HaroldRosenthal)

Mickey Mantle and Billy Pierce of the American League and Hank Aaron and Don Newcombe of the National

League! This glittering foursome won the Outstanding Player honor of the Sporting News for the 1956 season. They were selected in a poll of over 200 sports writers of major league cities. These honors are distinctive from the Most Valuable Player selections made by the Baseball Writers' Association of America that are to be announced later in the fall.

Mantle of the Yankees was chosen the number one player and the White Sox' Pierce the number one pitcher in the AL, while Aaron of the Braves won the accolade as the top NL player and Newcombe as the best pitcher.

It was Robin Roberts thirtieth birthday, and Manager Mayo Smith stuck with him all the way in search of his twentieth win of the season. To many observers, Roberts seemed nervous and tense as he went to the mound against the lowly Giants on the last day of the season.

Roberts lost his last chance to become a 20 game winner for the seventh consecutive season, a feat that was last accomplished by Lefty Grove back in 1930. Instead of winning his twentieth, Roberts went down to his eighteenth defeat.

Seven of Roberts' defeats came by the margin of a single run, four by scores of 2-1.

The Dodgers clinched a tie for the National League pennant and climbed to within one game of a second successive flag when they took a double-header from the Pirates in Brooklyn on Saturday, September 29, the next to last day of the season. The Brooklyn boys won by the score of 6-2 and 3-1 getting route going performances from Sal Maglie and Clem Labine.

Sandy Amoros, Gil Hodges and Carl Furillo all homered in the opener to back Maglie, who was making his first start after his no-hitter.

In the nightcap, Labine scattered seven hits, and received RBI help from Gil Hodges with a two run double. Roy Campanella also homered for the Bums. Roberto Clemente had three of the seven hits for the Buccos.

Friday and Saturday night were unpleasant for the Braves in St. Louis as they dropped consecutive decisions to the Cardinals and fell a full game behind the Dodgers going into the last day of the season.

After losing a 5-4 decision on Friday, the Braves were handed a second damaging defeat in as many nights when the Cardinals defeated Warren Spahn 2-1 in a twelve inning thriller.

Spahn and the Cardinal's Herm Wehmeir both went the distance in a game marked by spectacular defensive plays. Spahn held the Redbirds hitless until the sixth inning when they had back to back doubles from Don Blasingame and Alvin Dark.

The Redbirds won it in the bottom of the twelfth inning, when Stan Musial doubled with one out, Ken Boyer was intentionally passed and Rip Repulski doubled down the line off Eddie Matthews' glove.

Tears streamed down the face of the Braves' Spahn as he trudged from the mound at Busch Stadium after the game winning hit by Repulski. Emotion welled up in Spahn. As he walked off the field, his face reflecting his grief, an Associated Press photographer snapped a picture and the 35 year-old pitcher threw his glove at the newsman.

"Later in the clubhouse, Spahn apologized to the photographer. "I'm sorry, Buddy. I didn't want you to take that picture."

Manager Fred Haney and Spahn both went over to Eddie Mathews, who had failed to come up with Repulski's blazing liner that scored Stan Musial with the winning run. Mathews, too, was close to tears. His knee was red where the ball had struck him. Haney and Spahn shook hands with him, but little was said.

Meanwhile, General Manager Frank Lane of the Cardinals inquired if it were true that Spahn had cried after his loss to the Redbirds. Told that it was indeed true, Lane said: "What the hell do they expect him to do after losing a game like that, whistle!"

On Sunday, the last day of the season the Dodgers captured their second straight pennant by defeating the Pirates 8-6, with an outburst of five home runs, including the forty-second and forty-third by Duke Snider, who set a new Dodger record. Sandy Amoros also hammered two homers, while Jackie Robinson added one.

The slugging enabled Don Newcombe to earn his twenty-seventh win of the season, although he was not around at the finish. Don Bessent finished up for the Dodgers, as Newcombe was kayoed in the eighth inning.

The Braves, who muffed their chance to win the pennant when they dropped the two games in St. Louis, managed to win the season finale by the score of 4-2, as Lew Burdette won his nineteenth game. Eddie Mathews' two run homer was the decisive blow for the Braves, who finished one game behind the pennant winning Dodgers.

Scenes ranging from wild jubilation to quiet dignity greeted reporters when they stepped into the Dodger clubhouse following the pennant-clinching victory over the Pirates.

While Don Newcombe, clad in pink shorts, engaged in an impromptu dance, a more serious Carl Furillo remarked how he had prayed "as never before" for a Dodger victory.

At another spot, Duke Snider, whose two homers had earned for him a new club record of 43 round-trippers for the season, quietly sipped a bottle of champagne. "This has to be the greatest day for me," he observed.

Sandy Amoros, the Dodger "goat" only a few days earlier when his muff of a fly ball cost the club a victory, was perhaps the happiest of the lot. The Cuban Comet kept repeating constantly in Spanish, "Nice day, nice day."

The Yankees, resting and readying for the World Series, dropped a 7-4 decision to the Red Sox in their season finale. Mickey Mantle, who drove in a run as a pinch-hitter in the ninth inning, sewed up the Triple Crown with 130 RBI's, 52 homers and a .353 batting average. Yogi Berra added his thirtieth home run of the season in the first inning.

The Bronx Bombers finished nine games ahead of second place Cleveland with a 97-57 record.

Call him genius, clown, master-strategist, lucky or whatever you wish, but there's no denying Ole' Casey. Casey Stengel gets the job done! This is his seventh American League Championship as Yankee manager.

Billy Hoeft of the Detroit Tigers, in search of win number twenty, was the losing pitcher on Friday night against the Cleveland Indians, but bounced back in relief on Sunday to win his twentieth game of the season. Hoeft and teammate Frank Lary are only the third duo in major league history to win twenty games in a season for a second division club.

Bob Feller was the losing pitcher for the Indians, going the distance and dropping his record to 0-4. It was the first time in his illustrious career that Feller did not win a game during the season. In nine innings of work, Feller gave up eleven hits and did not strike out a batter.

The fabulous career of "Rapid Robert" Feller had come to an end! This would be his last major league game in a career that spanned three decades. In December, a few months later, Feller would announce his retirement from the game. His number nineteen was immediately retired by the Indians. An eight time All-Star, Feller pitched his entire 18 year career with Cleveland, hurling three no-hitters, winning 262 games and setting many strikeout records. He was a true champion, and described by many players as "the best pitcher of our era." He served four years in the United States Navy during the prime years of his career.

In his first career start August 23, 1936, Feller started against the St. Louis Browns and struck out 15 batters. A month later, he struck out 17 Philadelphia A's. He was seventeen at the time, and after his first summer of major league baseball, he returned to Van Meter, Iowa to begin his senior year of high school.

Bob Feller was a wonderful gentleman and a great ambassador for baseball. This writer had the privilege of chatting with him on several occasions later in his life, when the Cleveland club was holding spring training in Winter Haven, Florida.

The season-long drum-beating about his assault on Babe Ruth's record never bothered Mickey Mantle, but the Triple Crown, which he finally did win, really got under his skin.

"That last week or so I was very conscious of it," Mickey recalled. "To tell you the truth, I even dreamed about it at night and thought about it a lot. The last few days I kept telling myself I had better not get into another fuss like this, because it surely was nerve-wracking."

About the Ruth hullabaloo, he says: "I haven't even been thinking about hitting sixty homers for most of the season. When I missed four games before the All-Star Game, that's when I said to myself that I didn't think I could make it."

Although they finished in seventh place on the last day of the season, the Pittsburgh Pirates seemed to be making the turnaround they had all envisioned. Just a week before the end of the season, the Buccos were seemingly entrenched in sixth place, certain to escape the cellar where they had finished four consecutive years.

Forbes Field saw 950,000 fans go through the turnstiles, witnessing strong improvement in the club's play. Bill Virdon and Roberto Clemente finished in the top four in the National League batting race, and Bob Friend had an excellent year, especially his pitching against the top division clubs. Friend finished with a 17-17 mark.

Pirate right-hander, Vern Law was on the cusp of becoming a premier pitcher. In the next four seasons he would win 62 games for the Bucs, including the 1960 National League Cy Young Award.

The Pirates were a happy club. They played every game to the hilt, and Manager Bobby Bragan's fiery leadership had much to do with the Bucs success on the field as well as at the gate. The Pirates took their cue from Bragan and they were a relaxed team right down to the finish.

Bragan himself gets a kick out of relating many of the stories that came to pass during the 1956 season.

There was the day Roberto Clemente, the Puerto Rican who doesn't understand much English, tried to bunt in the eighth inning against the Dodgers with the Pirates trailing by a run at Ebbets Field.

Clemente was out, and after the game Bragan asked him his reason for bunting. "Why didn't you shoot for the seats, since a home run would have tied the score?" Bragan asked Clemente.

Clemente shook his head. "Tired, no feel like home run," he answered. "Why not swing away then?" Bragan pursued. "You might have punched out another double and would have been in a position to score."

"No good," Clemente replied. "Already have two doubles."

Bragan just grinned and threw up his hands.   (J. G. T. Spink)

It is interesting to note the extreme youthfulness of some of the top players. Hank Aaron, at twenty-two, is two years younger than Mickey Mantle and together, the pair promises a brilliant future, both for themselves and for the game.

Hank, who is an outfielder, the same as Mantle, doesn't pack quite as much home run power. He is more of a line drive hitter. But he is unquestionably the greatest hitter in the National League right now.

Hank Aaron reached his present high estate in just five years of professional baseball, starting in the Braves' farm system at Eau Claire, Wisconsin, in 1952. Averaging .328 this year, he won the NL batting title just five seasons later.

Hank, a quiet, modest fellow, hit .280 in his first year with Milwaukee in 1954 and.314 last season. His improvement is so rapid with each succeeding season that he may dominate the league henceforth just as Stan Musial has done in seasons past.

Dale Long's tremendous feat of hitting eight home runs in eight consecutive games will go down as the most spectacular feat of the 1956 season, even surpassing Mickey Mantle's effort to surpass Babe Ruth's season home run record.

The biggest pitching surprise of the season would be the three no-hitters all by veteran pitchers who age-wise should have seen their better days. Sal Maglie of the Dodgers, Carl Erskine of the Dodgers and Mel Parnell of the Red Sox, each shone brightly in the twilight of their career.

The most unusual development pitching wise during the season is that the Yankees won the American League pennant without a single twenty game winner. Three of the next four clubs, Cleveland, Chicago and Detroit all had at least one twenty game winner. It is somewhat surprising that the Indians with Bob Lemon, Early Wynn and Herb Score each winning twenty, did not even come close to winning the pennant.

The best home run comment came when the Los Angeles Angels put a $200,000 price tag on Steve Bilko. One major league general manager questioned: "which Bilko are they talking about, Steve or the Sergeant on television? At that price, if it's Bilko they are talking about, I'm not interested. If it's the Sarge, I am!" He was referencing the popular television show, Sergeant Bilko.

Seven members of the Yankees and a former Bomber will work out of Atlanta this winter, as employees of the United American Life Insurance Company. They are Tom Sturdivant, Jerry Coleman, Joe Collins, Mickey McDermott, Billy Hunter, Tommy Byrne and Charley Silvera, plus Phil Rizzutto, who was released in August.

The game must spruce up its parks if it hopes to retain the

interest of female fans, Leo Durocher suggested. The former manager of the Dodgers and Giants, now an NBC-TV executive, said. "I think women want to go to games, but they won't go to filthy parks and in too many cases facilities haven't been kept up with the times. Parks are better now than they used to be. There was a time when a woman wouldn't dare to go near one. But the club owners have got to do more. If they don't, it's going to hurt the game."

Two clubs have announced price increases for the upcoming 1957 season. The Tigers announced that reserved seats at Briggs Stadium next year would cost $2, an increase of twenty-five cents, and box seats will be priced at $3, up fifty cents. Bleacher and unreserved grandstand seats will remain unchanged at 75 cents and $1.25, respectively.

The Pirates will have a new price scale for Forbes Field, with the following increases: General admission from $1.40 to $1.50, reserved seats from $2.20 to $2.40 and box seats from $2.75 to $3. Prices for bleacher seats were not changed.

Walter O'Malley, President of the Dodgers, dashed any hopes that the metropolitan city of Los Angeles, California might land the Brooklyn club by announcing that the Dodgers definitely will remain in Brooklyn.

O'Malley said: "Wherever I go, whether it's Montreal, Dallas or Los Angeles, I'm asked about the possibility of shifting the Dodger franchise. We are going to get a new park in Brooklyn shortly and the Dodgers will definitely not be shifted." Dodger fans should have been advised to stay tuned on this one.

Major league players could use some batting lessons, says Ty Cobb, who thinks modern day hitters stand too far from the plate and make it easy for the pitchers to get them on outside pitches.

Cobb, now a Californian, made his observations following a recent trip to Baltimore, where he took part in a Hall of Fame celebration.

"If what I saw during the game between the Orioles and the Tigers was a good sample of major league ball, then the boys who play it can sure use some batting lessons," the Georgia Peach said.

"I noticed that most of them were arm swingers," he added. "They don't get any body into their swings because they stand so far away from the plate they have to reach for the ball. On pitches that cut the outside corners for strikes they might as well be in the clubhouse for all the chance they have of hitting the ball.

The Minor Leagues
(Down on the farm)

Ranked as one of the strongest teams to represent Los Angeles in the Pacific Coast League, the 1956 edition of the Angels clinched the club's first pennant since 1947 when they defeated Seattle, on September 4.

The Angels also have a chance at sweeping most of the individual awards in the PCL. Steve Bilko appears a cinch to be named the MVP, with teammate Gene Mauch expected to be the runner-up.

With less than two weeks remaining in the season, Bilko was the PCL leader in batting average (.363), home runs (53), runs batted in (155) and hits (201).

In the International League, Luke Easter, veteran Buffalo first baseman, paced the league in both home runs (39) and runs batted in (103), while Montreal's Clyde Parris edged Rochester's Joe Cunningham for the batting title, .321 to .320. Cunningham had three hits on the final day of the season, but Parris went two for four to maintain a slight edge. .

Dick Stuart, the Western League's 1956 strong boy, belted his way into fourth place in the all-time Organized Baseball homer standings during the campaign.

The 23-year-old Lincoln outfielder-first baseman smashed

four-bagger number 66 on the final day of the regular season against Topeka.

Stuart was being challenged by Ken Guettler, Shreveport outfielder (Texas League). Five days before the close of the Texas League schedule, Guettler had belted 62 homers. Slowed during the final week of the season with a groin injury, Guettler did not add another homer, but added a couple RBI's to finish with a league leading 143.

Jim McManus, Durham first baseman (Carolina League) was fined $10 and costs in Municipal County Court at Greensboro, September 4, on charges arising from a fight with a spectator there. McManus appeared in court with his hand in a cast as a result of an injury suffered in the melee.

The Houston Buffs split up their $5,000 prize for finishing first in the Texas League at a meeting on September 10. All 18 players on the roster, the team manager, Harry Walker and the team trainer, and clubhouse staff each received $208.09 apiece.

Lower minor leagues continued to struggle financially and at the gate. The Western League clubs suffered an average loss of about $17,000 for the '56 season, following a survey of the Class A circuit.

The Class C Evangeline League cancelled the final round of their playoff series, due to "declining interest and poor attendance," on September 11, stated league President Ray Mullins. After ten games in the two semi-final rounds, the league had only attracted a total of 5,197 paid admissions.

It's time for the minor leagues to start realigning by abolishing B, C and D classifications for leagues, says Dutch Hoffman, president of the Class D Midwest League.

"Put all the players from these classifications in one group," he said, "and then let the parent team distribute the talent among its clubs. Sure, we have rookies in all the classifications, but we would not be putting a stamp on one group of clubs, such as a Class D."

"We know that a Ford is not in the class with a Lincoln," Hoffman added, "but Ford doesn't advertise that it isn't. It should be the same way with us. Just because we don't have major league ball in the smaller cities is no reason to brand our product as inferior."

"We need to fix the minor leagues," he continued. Hoffman declares Organized Baseball advertises its products as being inferior when it brands a club B, C or D. (Howard Millard)

When the Omaha Cardinals ran wild for 28 hits to beat the Denver Bears 22-3 in the second game here in Denver, September 12, it was too much for the Grizzlies. "The boys felt a deep humiliation over that one and got mad," explained Manager Ralph Houk.

Denver's anger over the situation went up several degrees the next night at Omaha when a near free-for-all followed several incidents. The Bears thought that the Cardinal pitcher Frank Barnes was throwing at them, especially at Tony Kubek. When Kubek hit a ground foul in the fourth inning, Tommy Lasorda, Denver pitcher who was coaching at first base, picked it up and fired it at Barnes' shins.

Barnes evaded the throw and Third Baseman Stan Jok of Omaha retrieved the ball and threw it into the Denver dugout. Players from both benches then rushed to the mound uttering threats.

Two pitches later Kubek bunted down the first base line. He lowered his shoulder and made an attempt to block Barnes coming over to field the ball. That brought on another mob scene! Order again was restored with no blows struck, but Kubek and Barnes were both banished. Ed Doherty, American Association league president, subsequently fined each $25 and docked Lasorda and Jok $10 apiece. (Frank Haraway)

Because the Marlins had their backs to the wall in the International League playoffs, a challenge duel between Carlos Paula, a late-season team addition, and Leroy (Satchel) Paige) failed to materialize.

On the club's flight back from Rochester on September 14, Paula commented to Paige: "Old man, you don't throw balls hard like last time I saw you peetch."

"In the first place you ain't never seen me pitch before," Paige retorted. "In the second place, Ah can throw hard enough to get a nothing hitter like you out any day."

Paula was all for having a duel before a game. Satch was willing too, but when Miami lost the series in five games, the duel never came off. (Jimmy Burns)

Final Pacific Coast League statistics saw Steve Bilko make a clean sweep with all of the hitting honors. Bilko finished with a .360 average, 55 home runs, 163 RBI's, and 215 hits, all four categories were league leaders.

Houston fans rewarded their Texas League champions with gifts. Members of the Buff team were presented $120 each as the result of funds raised by an appreciation committee. Manager Harry Walker was given an automobile air conditioner.

CHAPTER SEVEN

The PERFECT World Series
(Final Standings on October 1, 1956)

American League				National League			
Team	**W**	**L**	**GB**	**Team**	**W**	**L**	**GB**
New York	97	57	---	Brooklyn	93	61	---
Cleveland	88	66	9	Milwaukee	92	62	1
Chicago	85	69	12	Cincinnati	91	63	2
Boston	84	71	13	St. Louis	76	78	17
Detroit	82	72	15	Philadelphia	71	83	22
Baltimore	69	85	28	New York	67	87	26
Washington	59	95	38	Pittsburgh	66	88	27
Kansas City	52	102	45	Chicago	60	94	33

No other sports event stirs up as much interest as the World Series. Through radio and television, the big diamond classic is brought into millions of living rooms, not only in the United States, but in Canada, Mexico, Cuba, Venezuela and our other Latin neighboring countries to the South.

Television in particular brings the World Series closer to the general public than ever before. Series play has provided its heroics as well as its heartaches. There have been Series heroes and Series goats. World Series have pulled down big names and made household words of obscure diamond figures.

The 1956 World Series began on Wednesday, October 3 at Ebbets Field in Brooklyn, followed by game two on Thursday. The series will move to the Bronx and Yankee Stadium for games three, four and five, before returning to Flatbush for the final two games, if necessary.

The crisp blue October sky and the multi-colored bunting that adorns every wall in Yankee Stadium and Ebbets Field signifies that autumn is upon us, and the World Series is set to begin.

Downtown stores and shops on Main Street, U.S.A., as well as classrooms in almost every elementary and high school in America are tuned in either by radio or television to the fall spectacle.

Two of the greatest sports voices of all-time, Mel Allen and Vince Scully lend their charismatic charm to each black and white television, while Bob Wolff and Bob Neal fill the airwaves on radio.

All of the Series games will start at 1:00 p.m. each day, except on Sunday, when the first pitch will be at 2:00 p.m.

GAME ONE! The fifty-third World Series began on a cool, but beautiful, sunshiny autumn day. The President of the United States, Dwight D. Eisenhower, participated in a World Series opener to such an extent that he was a co-attraction. The 34,479 fans first paid homage to Ike before the Dodgers got around to the pleasant task, for them, of "whomping" the Yankees 6-3.

As the game wore on, Sal Maglie, a weather-beaten 39 year-old pitcher, became the center of attraction.

On this day, he had been given the assignment ahead of Don Newcombe, Brooklyn's 27-game winner. Sal was the right man for the job though this seemed doubtful when

Mickey Mantle, in the first inning, hit his fifty-third home run of the season, a two-run jolt over the friendly right field wall. The Yankees, slight favorites to regain the world championship from their opponents, had Maglie close to a knockout more than once thereafter.

When the gates were opened at 10 a. m., there was no great rush for standing room tickets. It was possible for a fan to buy his way into the park right up to game time. In fact, odd-lot strips of reserved and box seats for the Ebbets Field part of the Series were being sold over the counter.

When Casey Stengel and Walt Alston posed for photographers, the Ole' Perfesser cautioned the camera men, "Careful with those flashlights, last year you blinded me so I didn't know what I was doing and we lost three here."

The appearance of President Dwight Eisenhower at the opening game of the World Series was the first visit of a chief executive to a classic game since 1936, when Franklin D. Roosevelt attended the game between the Yankees and Giants.

All the scoring on this inaugural day was accomplished in the first four innings. Thereafter there were threats, but Maglie for the winners and the three hurlers who followed Whitey Ford for the Yankees, Johnny Kucks, Tom Morgan and Bob Turley, kept the goose-eggs growing on the big scoreboard in right-center. The sixth run came off Kucks in the fourth inning.

Each team had nine hits, each team had two homers.

In the first inning, Dodger manager, Walt Alston must have wondered if he had sent the right man out to do the job. There was one out when Enos Slaughter, a year Maglie's senior and, like Sal, a castoff, got a single when his grounder took a bad bounce and got away from Gil Hodges. Mantle, with one strike and hitting from the left side, drove a homer high and far over the right field wall and out onto Bedford Avenue.

Then the fans saw the real Maglie. After Yogi Berra drew

a walk, Bill Skowron and Gil McDougald both went down swinging against the Barber.

Ford had no trouble with the Dodgers in the first inning, but the second was a different story. With a one ball, one strike count, Jackie Robinson slammed his second World Series homer, a robust shot in the lower left-center field seats. In no time at all the score was tied at 2-2 when Hodges singled and scored on a double to left by Carl Furillo.

The Dodgers finished Ford in the third inning. There was one out when Pee Wee Reese, in his sixteenth season, beat out a softly hit ball to deep short. Duke Snider followed with a single to center. Robinson flied out to Mantle, before Hodges blasted a three-run homer into the left field seats.

In the fourth, Billy Martin homered for the Bombers, but Brooklyn snatched that run back in their half of the inning, when Roy Campanella doubled and scored on a single by Sandy Amoros.

Maglie continued his mastery, as he finished the ninth with a flourish. Starting it off, he whiffed Hank Bauer, Slaughter singled to left for his third hit, but a moment later it was all over, when Junior Gilliam started a double play on Mantle's hard smash.

Maglie's ten strikeouts in the game marked a season high for the veteran hurler. (Ed Prell)

Game one goes to the Brooklyn Dodgers, with a 6-3 victory over the New York Yankees.

GAME TWO! The longest nine-inning game in World Series history, and one of the zaniest, ended with the Dodgers on top 13 to 8 for their second consecutive victory over the dazed American League champions. It was the first time the Dodgers ever had taken the first two matches in the fall classic. Likewise, the Yankees had never lost the first two.

The postponement of the second game because of rain, marked the first time that weather had interfered with the World Series since 1951.

This was a game which had to be seen to be believed and it's entirely possible the television viewers might have suspected they were being shown an old baseball comedy picture, not a World Series game.

The Yankees, after scoring once in the first inning off Don Newcombe, battered him for five runs in the second inning, a grand-slam homer by Yogi Berra knocked out Newk for his fourth failure in four Series starts.

Brooklyn came right back in the bottom half of the second, disposed of Don Larsen and continued their attack on Johnny Kucks and Tommy Byrne which netted the six tying runs. Three runs came on Duke Snider's homer off Byrne, the Duke's tenth and tying him with Lou Gehrig as all-time runner-up to Babe Ruth, who swatted fifteen.

The 21 runs scored were one short of tying a record for most runs in one game by two teams. The use of seven pitchers by the Yankees was an all-time high for one club, as were the 11 walks they issued. The four runs knocked in by Gil Hodges gave him seven for the two games, only two short of the record for one World Series set by Lou Gehrig.

Both teams had twelve hits during the contest, but the two runs scored in both the fourth and fifth innings by the Dodgers, pretty much settled the outcome, as they led 11 to 7 after five innings of play.

There were twenty-four base hits, twelve bases on balls, and eighteen runners left on base during the game, but the key to the Dodgers win and a commanding 2-0 lead in the Series would be the outstanding pitching by Dodger reliever, Don Bessent. In his seven inning relief job, Bessent held the American leaguers to two runs and only six hits in putting the Brooklyn's into a commanding position in the Series.

When some of his Yankees gathered around the cage to watch the Dodgers batting practice, Manager Casey Stengel chased his players away. "I don't want them snooping too close and I don't want you to do it, either," he told his men.

Before the opening game, a number of Dodgers had crowded around the cage to look over the Yanks and Stengel had ordered them off. Some of the Dodgers were reluctant to comply, whereupon Casey added, "You birds act like you own this park. Now get away."

It was Don, Don and Don. It was Don Newcombe for the Dodgers, Don Larsen for the Yankees and Don Bessent for the Dodgers, the winning pitcher in this one.

Hank Bauer, who was shifted from first to sixth in the Yankee batting order for the second game, was asked if the move surprised him. "I've been with Casey for eight years," Bauer replied, "and no lineup change will ever surprise me."

The twenty-five year old Don Bessent had pitched as much as seven innings of relief only once before. He relied mostly on his fast ball against the Bombers. He touched a high point in the game in the fourth inning when, he whistled three called strikes inside and knee high, to fan Mickey Mantle.

When questioned by reporters about what he may have said to his players after the two losses, Casey Stengel had a quaint reply to their questions, "I didn't kiss any of them and they didn't kiss me!"

GAME THREE! The Yankees, on the throngs of desperation, returned to Yankee Stadium for games three, four and five.

Enos (Country) Slaughter, 40 years old, who has been playing professional ball for over twenty years, gave the Yankees' first victory of the Series a story-book touch on October 6. A lot of fans probably wondered what Slaughter was doing in a Yankees uniform anyway? They had lost track of old Country after he had been sent away by the Cardinals at the start of the 1954 season. He was with the Yankees that year, which was distinguished by the fact the Bombers lost the pennant race to Cleveland. In 1955 old Enos wound up with Kansas City. Recently, just a week before the World Series rosters were frozen, the Yankees bought Slaughter back from the Athletics on August 25. It was as if, "you go play for the Athletics, and when we need you for the World Series, we will buy you back."

In the sixth inning of game number three, the Yankees and Whitey Ford were trailing Roger Craig and the Dodgers 2-1. At this point the 73,977 fans in Yankees Stadium were getting a little nervous and very unhappy. There were two out and two runners on base when Slaughter, with the count three balls and one strike, clubbed a homer into the lower right-field seats. Ford held on for a 5-3 victory and the Yankees had eliminated the thought of four straight defeats.

For the third straight game the hits were even, each team making eight. Ford gave the Yankees their first complete pitched game and did much to straighten out the staff which had been jumbled in the first two games, when a total of eleven pitchers were sent to the mound. Ford whiffed seven, getting Duke Snider three times.

Slaughter had hit two previous World Series homers, both with the Cardinals, one in 1942 and another in 1946. In the '46 Series, Slaughter homered against the Red Sox, but more importantly, he scored the winning run in the final game from first base on a single by Harry Walker. This was the play so often talked about in which Johnny Pesky, the Red Sox shortstop, held the ball briefly before throwing to the plate. By then, Enos was across the plate and the World Series was over.

Even the Slaughter blow didn't kill the Dodgers. Trailing 4-2, they came back in the seventh when Gil Hodges walked and hustled to third when Carl Furillo drove a single off the glove of Ford. Hodges then scored on a ground out to make the score 4-3.

The Yanks added a fifth run, an unearned one, in the eighth inning.

Ford picked up his fourth career World Series win, going the distance, allowing only three hits, while striking out seven.

In contrast to the three-hour and 26 minute (3:26) record-breaker the day before, the third game of the Series was run off in only two hours and seventeen minutes (2:17).

A variation in regulations between the two leagues showed up in the first inning when Roger Craig received a new ball from Plate Umpire Dusty Boggess and tossed it to Jackie Robinson, who began to rub it vigorously. Hank Soar of the American League, umpiring at third, took the ball from Robinson and tossed it out of the game. AL rules permit only the pitcher or the catcher to rub up the ball. The National League permits any player to rub it.

Yogi Berra said Whitey Ford's fast ball was alive, whereas in his first start in Brooklyn, "he threw nothing." Ford in discussing his performance, said, "I made three bad mistakes with location of the fast ball that would have beaten me in Brooklyn, playing in a smaller park. They were to Reese, Campanella and Furillo. But this ball park helped me."

GAME FOUR! The Series was beginning to look much like 1955 in reverse when the Yankees, behind their gifted 26-year old right-hander, Tom Sturdivant, whipped the Dodgers 6-2 to even the Series at two games apiece on a Sunday afternoon.

Sturdivant disclosed that he had taken a sleeping pill, "the first in my life," early the night before the game after he had learned that he was to start against the Dodgers. "I knew it would be impossible for me to sleep," he said. "Here I was, a nobody, starting the first Series game in my life. So I swallowed a pill at eight-thirty last night and didn't wake up until nine o'clock this morning. That guaranteed me enough sleep."

Carl Erskine, the Dodger starter was making his eleventh career World Series appearance, seeking to become the first Dodger pitcher to win three World Series games. He had won one game in 1952 and won another in '55, when he set the Series record of fourteen strikeouts in his 3-2 victory over the

Yankees.

Sturdivant had help from his teammates, who for the third time in the Series scored a run in the first inning. The Dodgers tied the score in the fourth, but the Yankees nailed Erskine for two runs in the bottom of the inning for a 3-1 lead.

Later, Mickey Mantle swatted a tape measure home run, a 440-footer high into the right-center bleachers, and Hank Bauer, playing in his thirty-sixth Series game, finally found the range with a runner on base to complete the scoring. Mantle's homer, his seventh in these skirmishes, was his second of the Series. Bauer's homer came off Don Drysdale, the 20-year-old bonus rookie from Van Nuys, California, who pitched the final two innings.

Sturdivant's clutch six-hit pitching job, which included seven strikeouts mixed with six walks, was applauded by the raucous crowd of 63,705.

Casey Stengel went to the mound twice in the ninth inning, but did not remove Tom Sturdivant, departing each time with an encouraging pat for the young right-hander. In the clubhouse, after the game, Sturdivant's first words to Stengel were: "Thanks for leaving me in skipper." Casey replied, "Thanks to yourself for getting us even."

GAME FIVE! The World Series of 1956 was viewed with apathy when the Yankees and Dodgers were set to meet for October's Big Apple. It was getting to be old stuff, same teams playing almost year after year. Any feelings of apathy were completely wiped out on the sunny afternoon of October 8, when the Series crowd of 64,519 in Yankee Stadium was about to witness the most famous World Series game ever played.

The boys from Brooklyn had won the first two games in Ebbets Field, while the Yankees had rallied to win two in their own park. Now the teams were battling for the edge which would put one or the other only a game away from the world championship.

All eyes were on Sal (The Barber) Maglie, a 39 year old wizard who had pitched the Dodgers to a pennant in the closing weeks. He was having a resurgence of his career, after being told by the Giants and Indians that he was no longer needed. The Barber had whipped the Yankees in the opener, now he was ready to lead Brooklyn back to the Series lead.

Sal's opponent was Don Larsen, a six-foot four-inch right-hander, who had been essentially a failure with the old St. Louis Browns and the Baltimore Orioles. He had lost twenty-one games in one season with the Orioles, before the Yankees took him in a trade in the biggest player deal, numerically of all time.

Maglie, was the one who would surely, between the two, turn in the superlative pitching performance. Indeed, it seemed as if Maglie would be the master, until Mickey Mantle smashed a homer with two out in the fourth inning to break up a hitless battle between these two rivals.

Suddenly, all eyes focused on Larsen, as inning after inning, he cut down the Dodgers. Tension mounted, on the field and in the almost packed park, until the feat became a fact, a perfectly-pitched no-hitter, 27 batters up, 27 batters down!

Larsen mixing fast balls, curves and a slider in a delivery which had no windup, threw only 97 pitches. Only once was he in danger of issuing a walk, this when the count was 3-2 on Pee Wee Reese, the second batter of the game. After that he threw no more than two balls to any single batter. He fanned seven would be hitters, five of them in the first four innings and four of those were on called out strikes, as he continually baffled the Dodger hitters.

There were several sparkling plays that helped preserve the perfect game. Mantle raced deep into left-center for a back-handed grab of Gil Hodges' drive in the fifth, the longest ball hit by any Dodger. Jackie Robinson led off the second inning with a liner which caromed off Andy Carey's glove directly to

Gil McDougald, whose throw to first nipped Robinson by a half-step.

Brooklyn batters called Larsen's deliberate delivery "sneaky fast." Babe Pinelli, umpiring behind the plate for the last time in his long major league career, said he never saw two pitchers with such marvelous pin-point control. "Both Maglie and Larsen were hitting the corners with uncanny skill," said Pinelli

Mantle's homer and another run in the sixth inning wrapped up the scoring in the 2-0 game which went into the baseball record books as the all-time World Series classic.

The tension became tremendous in the ninth inning, as the crowd roared with every pitch from Larsen. He was aware that he had a no-hitter about the seventh inning. "I wasn't giving much thought to a no-hitter," said Don, "I was after the game first. We had to win."

After Carl Furillo had flied out to Hank Bauer leading off the Dodgers' ninth, and Roy Campanella grounded out to Billy Martin, Walter Alston sent up Dale Mitchell, to pinch-hit for Maglie. With the entire stadium in an uproar and on their feet, the first pitch to Mitchell was ball one, outside, strike one called, strike two swinging, foul to the left into the crowd, then, strike three called, as the right arm of Babe Pinelli thrust high into the air. Don Larsen had thrown only 97 pitches on the way to undying fame!

One of the more famous sports related pictures ever, was that of Yankee catcher, Yogi Berra leaping into the arms of Larsen, as teammates converged from every side to congratulate the hurler.

Don Larsen had just become the most astonishing hero in World Series history!

While downcast in defeat, the Dodgers were unanimous in their praise of Don Larsen. "He was just perfect, that's all," Pee Wee Reese declared. Jackie Robinson marveled at Larsen's "great control" and said, "It was the finest performance

I've ever seen."

The game played in two hours, six minutes (2:06), was the fastest Series contest since October of 1951, when the Yankees beat the Giants 3-1 in two hours, five minutes (2:05).

Manager Casey Stengel provided what was probably the best laugh of the year when he said one of the first newsmen to reach him after the no-hitter had asked very seriously, "Tell me, Mr. Stengel, do you think that was the best game Don Larsen ever pitched?"

Asked about his no windup delivery that he and teammate Bob Turley had adopted, Larsen replied, "I dug it up myself. On September 21 we opened our last series with the Red Sox in Boston. I had gotten the impression that Boston coach Del Baker had been stealing my stuff and I decided to stop it. I made up my mind to go to the no-windup."

"It has worked to perfection for me. How much more could I expect it to do for me? I fool the batters better. I have better control. I fool the Bakers. It's wonderful."

Casey Stengel believes that "Larsen's no-windup delivery, which he picked up last month in Boston, is sure to intrigue young pitchers, not only in the Little League class but in the majors as well," Casey declared. "The limited windup helps control, and I should think it would help youngsters. However, you have to have a strong arm to throw hard without a windup."

After having seen Larsen and Turley operate, Carl Erskine and Don Drysdale of the Dodger staff said they would go for that style of pitching in 1957, unless Walter Alston objected.

Alston told The Sporting News that he was not adverse to the experiment. (Dan Daniel, New York, N.Y.)

Don Larsen, a happy go lucky guy, who is known to not save much of what he makes, was in need of some financial relief, too.

Before the big right-hander had gone to the mound in the second Series game at Brooklyn and was knocked out, he had told close friends how desperately he wanted to win "for financial reasons," he exclaimed. "Golly, I need to beat them today. I've already spent the loser's share."

It was also revealed that shortly before he pitched his perfect game, Don had gone to Yankee road Secretary, Bill McCorry, trying to borrow $200 against his anticipated World Series check. McCorry said he had no authority to issue such a check, since Series money came out of the Commissioner's office.

"This is serious," Larsen reportedly told McCorry. "I have to get home to California and I don't have a nickel."

"You win today," McCorry said, "and I'll see that you get the $200."

After the perfect game, McCorry came to Larsen with a check for $200. "I don't need it now," the happy Larsen said. "I've already earned $2,000 since the game ended. Keep it!"

GAME SIX! When these two slugging teams came back to little Ebbets Field after the Yankees had won three straight in their own stadium, a free-hitting battle was anticipated. Bob Turley, the Yankee starting pitcher, himself, like Don Larsen, had been no ball of fire during the regular season, and had lasted only an inning and one-third in the third game of the 1955 Series in the same park. Clem Labine, the Dodger starter at best, was a gamble, too. Labine, whose eight previous World Series appearances had all been in relief roles, was about to establish himself as the newest star in this Series of stars.

Yes, this was a Series of surprises. This sixth game, won by the Dodgers by the minimum of margins, 1-0, was unforgettable in its own right. The biggest surprise was the tremendous pitching of Labine, a bull-pen guy who proved to be just the man to deadlock the fierce competition between these two great clubs.

Labine was not as spectacular as his strong-armed opponent, but he had more skill this day and much better control.

He struck out five and walked only two and one of those was intentional. Bob Turley, who like Don Larsen had abandoned the windup to his delivery, walked eight, including the two times he purposely passed Duke Snider. The Dodgers had seven hits off Turley, but each time he worked his way out of jams. He struck out eleven Dodger hitters.

The smallest crowd of the Series, 33,224, watched the ultimate pitching matchup, as the game was scoreless after nine innings. The Dodgers won it in the bottom of the tenth inning on a line drive base hit by Jackie Robinson.

Leading off the bottom of the tenth, Junior Gilliam walked on four straight balls from Turley. Pee Wee Reese then laid down a sacrifice bunt, bringing up Duke Snider. The Yankee strategy then dictated an intentional walk to Snider, his second of the day.

It brought up Robinson, who had left five runners stranded in three previous at-bats. He lined Turley's second pitch into left field, directly at Enos Slaughter. Battling the sun and increasing shadows, Slaughter charged the ball. Too late, he saw his mistake as the ball soared past him, just over his head and out of the reach of his outstretched glove to drive in Gilliam easily from second for the winning run.

"The ball took off and went over my head," Slaughter said. "When it was hit, I broke for it and thought I had a chance to catch it, but it suddenly zoomed upward and I never got my glove on it." He debunked the idea that he lost the ball in the sun. "The sun is only bad here in the early innings," he explained. "I did not need sun glasses for Robinson's ball. I saw it all the way, just didn't catch it."

Turley, who adopted the no-windup delivery used so successfully by Don Larsen, said he believed his effectiveness had been improved. "It makes me feel comfortable and relaxed," said the fireballer. "It could be the life-saver of my major league career."

Duke Snider said Bob Turley was the fastest pitcher the

Dodgers had faced this year. Roy Campanella agreed, saying: "All I know is Turley struck out eleven batters, including me three times. When you see me swishing and never even getting a foul tip, man, you know that pitcher is real fast."

A pitch-by-pitch count showed that Clem Labine served up 121 pitches and Bob Turley 141. Labine fired 78 strikes and Turley accounted for 83.

Umpire Larry Napp refused to permit Labine to sit down on second base after the Dodger pitcher had doubled in the eighth inning. Labine said, "I was tired and wanted to rest for a moment, but he told me to get up, that it was a 'bush' trick to sit down." Labine and Napp exchanged a few words, but he then resumed his feet.

Labine called his ten-inning 1-0 victory "the greatest thrill of my life. It was the longest and best game I ever pitched in the majors," said the Dodger relief ace turned starter, "and also the most important. Even that one back in 1951 wasn't as big.

Labine referred to his 10-0 victory over the Giants in the second game of the playoff series for the '51 National League pennant. He has been a relief pitcher almost exclusively during his career.

GAME SEVEN! Never in World Series play had the Yankees combined such devastating power and superlative pitching, as they rolled to a 9-0 victory over the Dodgers for their seventeenth world championship.

It was a resounding victory over the National League champions in the park where they had upended the Yankees six straight times in the battle for baseball's biggest prize, going back to the 1953 Series. It was a chilly and gloomy early October day and the Yankees performance put even more of a chill on the Dodger faithful.

The Yankee standouts were Yogi Berra, who slammed a pair of two run homers off Don Newcombe, and 23-year-old Johnny Kucks, who in his first Series start held the NL champs to three singles. Only 28 Dodgers officially came to the bat against Kucks, who walked three and only struck out one batter, Jackie Robinson. He was aided by two double plays. The Dodger bats were as cool and gloomy as the temperature in Ebbets Field.

This was becoming all too commonplace for Newcombe, as the gigantic right-hander whose 27 victories during the season represented the most important contribution of any pitcher for the league title. It was big Newk's fifth series start and his fourth knockout since he lost his debut, back in 1949, in a 1-0 duel, losing that one on a ninth inning homer by Tommy Henrich.

Berra's two homers against Newcombe in the payoff game before 33,782 chilled fans was all the more important because, preceding each of his homers, Mickey Mantle had struck out.

The job by Kucks climaxed an amazing form reversal by the Yankee staff, which had been brutalized in the first two matches in this park. Kucks route going performance was the fifth consecutive complete game against the Dodgers, following Whitey Ford, Tom Sturdivant, Don Larsen and Bob Turley, all going the distance.

Bill Skowron's seventh inning grand slam accounted for four of the Yankee runs, aided by two by Berra in the first inning, and again two more by Yogi's bat in the third. Elston Howard, who was playing for the first time in the Series as a replacement for Enos Slaughter, banged a solo homer in the fourth to send Newk to the showers, amidst boos banging against his ears.

Johnny Kucks, the Yanks' young right-hander, used a sinking fast ball and a slider to battle the Dodgers in his first Series start. The youngster was highly nervous before the biggest moment of his career. He took his turn in the batting cage, bunted several pitches and then was surrounded by a mass of photographers, who wanted him to pose with Newcombe. "No, no, let me alone," Kucks shouted as he fled into the dugout.

Flatbush fans knew it was all over when Bill Skowron hit his grand slam off Roger Craig in the seventh inning. They began leaving the park in droves and by the time the game ended, the stands were half-empty.

Bob Grim, the Yankees ace reliever, was the forgotten man of the Series. Manager Casey Stengel did not call on him in the first two games and the Yankees then came through with the five straight route going performances.

Although Duke Snider escaped striking out in the final game, he set a new record for most whiffs, in a total Series, when he fanned eight times in the first six games to bring his total to 33 for five World Series'. The former record was thirty by Babe Ruth who played in ten Series.

"I'm not talking about next year, but I'll let you in on a little secret," Casey Stengel told the writers, "I'm not worried about where I'll be next spring." Just two days after the Series, Casey signed a new contract to manage the Yankees for two more years, at $80,000 a year.

The Series finish just beat the cold weather. It was the nippiest day of all. Many of the reporters fled the stands for the warmth of the Ebbets Field press room, but the telegraphers, most of them operating old-fashioned Morse wires, had to keep pounding away at their keys.

The Yankees World Series victory touched off a celebration which ran close to dawn in the handsome surroundings of the Waldorf-Astoria's Starlight Roof, which earlier had been the Yankees headquarters. The several hundred participants included the players and their wives, the official family including Yankees scouts and minor league officials, and the newspaper and radio men who had traveled with the club during the successful campaign. (Harold Rosenthal)

Meanwhile, the Dodgers put on a small private "win or lose" party for newspapermen close to the club, office officials and representatives of the various farm clubs, following their collapse in the final game.

It was in the Madison Room of the Hotel Roosevelt and champagne flowed and not a tear was shed, as the Dodgers thoughts turned to their upcoming trip to Japan.

The world champion Yankees earned $8,714.76 apiece for their winning effort in the World Series and the Dodgers became the richest losers in the history of the classic by raking in $6,934.34 on the basis of each full share. The total player pool for this year's classic was $530,993.15 for the two competing clubs with the winners getting 60 percent and the losers 40 percent. (Carl Lundquist)

The Yankees cut up their pool into full shares for 32 people, including Manager Stengel, his three coaches, the trainer, road secretary and two players who were not with them for the Series, Phil Rizzuto, released, and Irv Noren, who had been on the disabled list much of the year. Enos Slaughter, who joined the team very late in the regular season, received three-fourths of a share.

The Dodgers had 28 full shares, including the manager, Walt Alston, his three coaches, and the trainer. The Dodgers did not include the traveling secretary because National League clubs are required by a league rule to give the secretary a full share.(Harold Rosenthal)

Don Larsen's signature came cheap as compared to the figures at which bonus babies are now receiving. "I don't remember just how much I got for signing, maybe $500," Larsen recalls, "but the St. Louis Browns gave me a little money when I signed, before they sent me to Aberdeen, South Dakota. That was a Class C League and they paid me $150 a month."

Several days later Don Larsen was asked how he spent the evening after pitching the perfect game. Don said, "Well, I met up with some buddies of mine from San Diego. We made the rounds of a few places and wound up at the Copa."

"A few beers?" he was asked.

Don smiled. "I like beer," he replied. "Besides, if I had a couple the night before the game, it stands to reason I'm going to have a couple the night after."

In baseball terms, the magnitude of Larsen's no-hitter cannot be described in just words, as history has to be a part of it all.

To do it against the tremendously talented Brooklyn Dodgers, the New York Yankees biggest rival makes it an even more incredible feat.

It had never happened before and is not likely to ever happen again. Baseball is a game of "learning how to deal with failure" even more than success. Don Larsen's last two starts during the 1956 World Series personifies that statement, as just a few days earlier in Game Two of the Series, he had failed to even complete two innings of work, as the Yankees fell to the Dodgers by the score of 13-8. Larsen gave up one hit, and walked four in a frustrating appearance. This time he was perfect.

Bob Hope was one of the first to entice Larsen to appear on his television show on NBC. Don is booked solid most of the upcoming winter. At this time last year, he was touring Japan as one of the Yankee group. And the winter before that, he worked in the stock room of Sears Roebuck in San Diego, "just to keep a little busy and make enough to pay a few bills."

For his appearance on the Hope show alone, Larsen received $7,500. He was awarded a new Corvette by Sport Magazine, as the outstanding player of the World Series. Supermarkets are besieging him for personal appearances at $1,000 a pop, and fashionable resorts throughout the country are requesting the pleasure of his presence.

When Larsen arrived on the NBC television set in Hollywood, he and Hope were posed for pictures with a well-formed spectacular sort of blonde named Diana Dors. Miss Dors was attired in the most attractive negligee this side of no negligee at all.

Hope and Larsen were asked to put their arms around Diana. Bob winked at Don and said: "We're off to a great start, aren't we kid?"

Don handled his punch lines beautifully. When Hope asked "I noticed that you shook off Yogi Berra's signs during your perfect game?"

"I wasn't shaking off any signs, I was just shaking," replied Don. "By the ninth inning I was there on the mound having my own private earthquake."

"Don, have you ever seen any little leaguers?" Hope asked.

"Sure. We played Cleveland," Larsen cracked, making reference to the fact that Bob Hope is a Cleveland Indians stockholder.

Larsen was asked afterward if he were making any particular plans for the future. He answered frankly: "I guess I'd like to save a little dough and go into business of some kind. I haven't anything specific in mind. "The most important thing right now is to keep on winning," adding with a grin: "A guy who doesn't win doesn't stay famous very long." (Melvin Durslag)

Accorded a tumultuous reception in traditional Hawaiian fashion, with hula girls extending the welcome of the islands, the Dodgers arrived in Honolulu by special Pan American Airways on October 12, and posted three straight victories before departing for Japan on their tour of the Pacific.

Once arriving in Japan, the Dodgers lost two of their first five exhibition games. The touring National League champions still were packing in Japanese fans and getting a big play in the press and on radio and television.

The first three games the Dodgers played in Tokyo drew approximately 85,000 to Korakuen Stadium. They lured another 35,000 in their 1-0 victory over the Yomiuri Giants at Sappporo on the island of Hokkaido and they played before 30,000 when the beat the All-Kanto Stars, 8-0 at Sendai, a few hundred miles north of Tokyo on October 24.

With the Yankees' undefeated record of last year here in mind, the Dodgers had hoped to make a clean sweep of all their games in Japan. "We'll be in there playing every minute," said Pee Wee Reese, "and we'll try to score as many runs as we can." But the major leaguers were rudely awakened, as they were feeble at bat. Two fantastic pitchers with the Yomiuri Giants, with amazing curve balls fanned 16 Dodgers.

The Dodgers, without attempting to alibi for their loss, praised the pitching and all-around performance of the Giants. "They just beat us," said Manager Alston. "They hit and we didn't. Those two pitchers threw some good curves. Heck, maybe that's over-simplifying it. They struck out 16. Anybody who strikes out sixteen has to be good." (Bob Bowie, Tokyo Japan)

Major league teams visiting the Orient in the future will find it more and more difficult to beat Japanese opposition, in the opinion of President Warren Giles of the National League, who left Tokyo to return to Cincinnati after accompanying the Brooklyn Dodgers on part of their tour.

"The improvement in Japanese baseball impressed me," Giles said, "and so did the hospitality, friendliness and enthusiasm of the Japanese people. Each year it is going to be harder and harder for the major league teams coming over here to win, because the Japanese have improved so much." (Bob Bowie)

Hopes of someday a major league team moving to Los Angeles did not die when the Senators' board of directors voted to continue operating in Washington.

"Someday a major league team will realize the value of moving here," said Kenneth Hahn, a member of the Los Angeles board of Supervisors and a leader in the campaign to get a team on the West Coast.

The owners of the Washington Senators will make no attempt to transfer their operation to another city, a decision which no doubt gratified thoughtful baseball people everywhere. But the lure and the excitement of Major League Baseball to the West Coast and to other cities like Minneapolis and Kansas City is imminent.

The sale of Ebbets Field, announced in late October, will not move the Dodgers out of the park they opened 43 years ago. Red Patterson, the Dodgers assistant general manager stated that, "The Dodgers fully intend to stay in Brooklyn. The lease with new ownership insures us home now until the new stadium can be built."

The deal of new stadium ownership is not expected to affect Brooklyn fans' attitude toward the Dodgers. Obsolete Ebbets Field, with a top capacity of 32,111, drew more than 1,200,000 during the recent 1956 season, second only to County Stadium in Milwaukee.

Minor Leagues/Barnstorming

Could the glory days of barnstorming teams be over? Despite summerlike weather, attendance proved disappointing for the first six games played by Spec Shea's Major League All-Stars on the barnstorming tour of the New England states. Crowds ranged from as little as 200 to a top of 1,000.

Shea said, "This probably will be the last year I'll take a team out on the road. Last year we had cold weather most of the time and the crowds were bigger than they are now. It's not worthwhile at all."

As a former Yankee and Senators pitcher, Shea declared that television was at fault. "The fans have become familiar with big league players during the season," he said. "Before television it was a novelty when big leaguers came to town. No more. Why, even the kids don't show up like they did before TV. They, too, see all the big leaguers they want during the season."

Shea's major leaguer barnstormers completed their schedule at Pawtucket, Rhode Island on October 21, with a disappointing 605 fans. Shea said following the game, "We drew so poorly, I'm sure I won't field a team next season. Financially, this was our worst trip."

Willie Mays and his Major League All-Stars, following the well-beaten path of Negro barnstormers, found the road rough at the start of their tour when attendance for their first seven games fell more than 50 per cent under the gates of previous years.

Opening at Charlotte, North Carolina, the All-Stars posted an 8-2 triumph before a slim turnout of 698 on a cool, clear, October 11 night.

Another small crowd of 558 was present in balmy weather in Nashville, Tennessee, when the major leaguers racked up their third victory on the tour.

The big leaguers of Mays' squad posted their twelfth straight victory at Montgomery, Alabama, October 24, winning 7-1, before only 696 paid in 65 degree weather. The club has drawn only a total of 14,843 paid fans, last year after twelve games, they had drawn 34,789 fans.

Times were changing. The fact that baseball was now available on television six months a year, was definitely affecting the barnstormers.

The shameful racial puzzle in Louisiana, specifically with the Texas League, reached new lows as league officials wrestled unsuccessfully with the new racial segregation law of Louisiana. The law will affect league play when the 1957 season opens.

The Louisiana law, which went into effect on the same day the Texas League held its meeting, says there shall be no mixed athletic contests in that state. It provides for penalties for each participant, from 60 days to one year in jail and a fine of from $100 to $1,000.

Most of the Texas League clubs said they would field the

best teams available and indicated they expect the teams to include Negro players. None of the clubs indicated it had any intention of breaking the Louisiana law, however, and league president, Dick Butler said, "Nobody is going into the courthouse."

Several clubs said they would ask Shreveport to withdraw from its lineup any player whose position corresponded to that usually played by any Negro on the visiting team.

For example, if Houston had a Negro shortstop, it would not be able to use him in games at Shreveport. Houston would ask Shreveport to bench its regular shortstop and use a substitute, in an effort to equalize playing strength.

But Bonneau Peters, the militant president of the Shreveport Sports, said he would not agree to any sort of compromise. "If these clubs want to play at Shreveport," he said, "they'll just have to play under the law of Louisiana. I'm not going to do anything about it."

The Houston Buffs will be the first team to go into Shreveport under the new Louisiana law, when they visit on April 16. Houston expects to have several Negroes on its team. The general manager of the Buffs said, "We will play the best players, regardless of color. We will not attempt to break the law but we will ask the league president to make a ruling that will even the competition (by substituting players on a position-for-position basis)."

Dallas and Austin took virtually the same stand as Houston. Tulsa and San Antonio said their clubs "will not be closed to Negroes" but would make no further comment.

Fort Worth said merely that it would respect the laws of Louisiana. Oklahoma City said it doubted it would have any Negro players on its roster but that if it did, it would not play them in Shreveport. (Bill Rives)

How difficult it must have been for the young Negro players playing in the Texas League and other similar leagues in 1956. In one sense, it was even more difficult than a decade earlier when Jackie Robinson broke the major league color barrier.

Baseball's Golden Season Revisited

Having seen their dynasty crumble in 1955, losing to their bitter crosstown rival, the Brooklyn Dodgers four games to three in the World Series, the New York Yankees had spent the winter with revenge on their minds. 1956 was to be the last of the all-New York Series until the year 2000, when the Yankees and Mets would meet. It was also the last time a New York based team represented the National League until the "Miracle Mets" of 1969 defeated the Baltimore Orioles.

The Yankees were World Series Champions five consecutive years from 1949-1953, but had missed out in '54, as the crosstown New York Giants took the Series from the Cleveland Indians.

The '69 Mets, as an expansion team had debuted only seven years earlier, in 1962 with a 120 loss season, ironically with the same Casey Stengel at the helm. In '69, the Mets defeated the Orioles in five games to one of what was to be one of the biggest upsets in professional sports history.

Part of the greatness of the 1956 major league baseball season was evident in that there were 24 eventual Hall of Famers on the Opening Day starting lineups of Major League Baseball's 16 teams. With several expansions through the next sixty years, it is doubtful that even with double the amount of players participating now in Major League Baseball, there may never be another single season that has as many Hall of Famers participating as in 1956, "Baseball's Golden Season."

In addition, to those who were starters on this day, there were numerous others who would eventually become Hall of Famers, including Bob Feller, Hoyt Wilhelm, Don Drysdale, Sandy Koufax, Bill Mazeroski and George Kell, all of whom were on MLB rosters during the '56 campaign, but were not in their team's Opening Day starting lineup.

There were also four MLB Executives, six managers, two umpires and Commissioner Ford Frick, each of whom were part of MLB during the '56 season, bringing the total to over 40 Hall of Famers involved in Major League Baseball in 1956.

The 24 Opening Day starters were, Ted Williams, Nellie Fox, Larry Doby, Bob Lemon, Al Kaline, Enos Slaughter, Yogi Berra, Mickey Mantle, Whitey Herzog, Duke Snider, Pee Wee Reese, Jackie Robinson, Roy Campanella, Ernie Banks, Monte Irvin, Frank Robinson, Eddie Mathews, Hank Aaron, Willie Mays, Richie Ashburn, Robin Roberts, Roberto Clemente, Red Schoendienst, and Stan Musial. Each of these gentlemen added to the greatness of the 1956 season.

IT IS VERY PROBABLE THAT THE GREATEST BASEBALL PLAYER THAT EVER LIVED MAY INDEED HAVE BEEN A PARTICIPANT IN "BASEBALL'S GOLDEN SEASON."

With the Dodgers winning in '55 behind Duke Snider's four home runs and MVP pitcher Johnny Podres' two complete games, it was time for the Yankees to return to glory. The previous years' Series also saw Jackie Robinson steal home, as the 1955 World Series title was the first in the Dodgers franchise history.

The city of New York had seen two consecutive National League teams come away with the Series. It was painful for the Yankee players and fans alike to have the world championship held by anyone other than the Bronx Bombers. The Dodgers had essentially won the '55 NL pennant early on as they were off to a 22-2 start, cruising to the flag. The Brooklyn's held a nine and one-half lead after three weeks and would never be challenged throughout the summer, as they won the pennant by thirteen and one-half games, before admonishing the Yankees in the '55 World Series.

It was a different story in 1956, as the Dodgers struggled for most of the season and actually led the league for only

10 days, with never more than a one and one-half game lead. The NL race went down to the last day of the season, as the Dodgers edged the Milwaukee Braves and Cincinnati Reds in one of the more dramatic pennant races ever. The opposite was taking place for the Yankees as they won 97 games in winning the American League pennant by nine games over the second place Cleveland Indians.

The Yankees were managed by Casey Stengel, who himself had been the Dodgers manager some years earlier. The Dodgers were managed by Walter Alston, who operated on 23 one year contracts during his long and successful Hall of Fame career.

The Yankees' Mickey Mantle was named the American League MVP, by winning the Triple Crown, the first to do so since Ted Williams in 1947. Mantle hit a league leading .353, with 52 home runs, and had 130 RBI's, while scoring 132 runs. In over 600 plate appearances, he only struck out 99 times, while he received 112 bases on balls. Ted Williams had emphatically stated during spring training that this would be the year that Mantle would emerge to super stardom.

Mantle barely edged a young Al Kaline of the Detroit Tigers in RBI, as Kaline had 128, almost depriving Mantle of the Triple Crown.

Harvey Kuenn of the Tigers led the American League in base hits with 196, while AL Rookie of the Year Luis Aparicio, of the Chicago White Sox also was the league leader in stolen bases with 21.

Eddie Yost of the Washington Senators earned the nickname as "The Walking Man." Yost received 151 bases on balls.

Herb Score, at age 23, pitching for the Cleveland Indians in only his second major league season struck out 263 batters, while winning 20 games.

Hank Aaron of the Milwaukee Braves continued to emerge as a rising star, as he led the National League in batting with a

.328 mark, while leading the league in base hits with 200.

Duke Snider of the Brooklyn Dodgers led the NL in home runs with 43, while the St. Louis Cardinals Stan "The Man" Musial was the league's RBI leader with 109. Snider, a feared hitter received 26 intentional bases on balls to lead the majors in that category.

The Giants, Willie Mays led the National League and all of baseball in stolen bases with 40.

Don Newcombe of the Dodgers was the NL MVP, as he won a prolific 27 games, while completing 18 of those contests, with 268 innings pitched, on the way to winning baseball's inaugural Cy Young Award (only one was given in '56)

Milwaukee's Lew Burdette posted an outstanding 19-10 record and was the NL leader with 2.70 ERA. The Chicago Cubs' "Sad Sam" Jones led the NL in strikeouts with 176

The two Rookies of the Year award winners were, Luis Aparicio of the AL Chicago White Sox and Frank Robinson in the NL, who represented the Cincinnati Redlegs (Reds).

There were many less significant debuts and retirements during the "Baseball's Golden Season." At 16 years, 10 months and one day, Jim Herrington of the Chicago White Sox became the youngest pitcher ever to start a Major League Baseball game. On September 30, two months prior to reaching the age of 17, the lanky lefty, Herrington hurled six innings against the Kansas City A's.

Dale Mitchell, an eleven year MLB veteran and a career .312 hitter, who would have been a borderline Hall of Famer had he played a bit longer. Mitchell retired from baseball after taking Don Larsen's final pitch in the perfect game for a called strike three. Mitchell, who always claimed the pitch was "high and outside," was not shy in later years about discussing the pitch. "Babe Pinelli, the home plate umpire retired after that pitch," said Mitchell. "He should have retired before the pitch."

Ralph Branca, the Dodger pitcher best remembered for

giving up the three-run ninth inning home run to the New York Giants Bobby Thomson in the final game of the 1951 National League playoff series, quietly retired after the '56 season. Branca pitched for 12 major league seasons compiling a creditable 88-68 record for three teams.

Bobby Thomson's "Shot Heard 'Round the World," on October 3, 1951, is right alongside Don Larsen's masterpiece as one of the greatest baseball games ever played.

Mel Parnell, the lefty who spent a decade with the Boston Red Sox, retired after the '56 season, with an impressive 123-75 record. Fenway Park was always known as a tough place to pitch for any left hander, but Parnell always performed well there, posting a 71-30 lifetime record.

Parnell remains the all-time winningest left-hander in Boston Red Sox history. In 1949, he won 25 games and had there been a Cy Young Award then, he would have certainly won it. The '49 season saw Mel break Babe Ruth's record for Red Sox wins in a season, surpassing the Babe's 24 wins. He was another who appeared to be on the Hall of Fame track, but a broken arm in spring training of 1954 curtailed his career and he was never the same afterward. However, he did have enough left during his final season to throw a no-hitter against the Chicago White Sox.

Another '56 retiree was Al "Flip" Rosen, who spent his entire 10 year career with the Cleveland Indians. Known as "Flip" and "The Hebrew Hammer," Rosen was the 1953 American League MVP and was a four-time All-Star. Rosen's amazing 1953 season was one for the record book, as he just missed the Triple Crown. He hit 43 home runs, had 145 RBI's, and hit .336, losing the AL Batting Title to Washington's Mickey Vernon who hit .337. He had a .285 career batting average and slugged 192 home runs, but is best known for his baseball executive career after retirement from active play. Rosen became President of the New York Yankees in 1978 and later for the Houston Astros. He quite possibly did his best work as President and General Manager for the San Francisco Giants from 1985-'92.

The 1956 season saw the debut of Curt Flood, who went on to have an outstanding 15 year major league career. However, Flood is most known for how he refused to be traded, thus modifying the Reserve Clause, which is known as the Curt Flood Rule. The rule states that when a player has played for a team for five straight years, and played in the MLB for a total of ten years, they have to give the club their consent to be traded.

Bill White made his major league debut in 1956 and had a very successful career beginning with the New York Giants. White played for four teams during his 13 year career, mostly with the St. Louis Cardinals. He hit 202 career home runs and had a .286 career batting average. He was an eight-time All-Star, seven-time Gold Glove winner and won a World Series in 1964 with the Cardinals. However, White is best known for becoming the first African American broadcaster for a Major League Baseball team, and later became the first African American to become President of a major sports league, when he assumed the duties as National League President.

At age 37, Ted Williams played in only 136 of the 154 Red Sox games but hit a lusty .345 in only 400 official at-bats. "The Splendid Splinter" actually had 503 plate appearances, receiving 102 bases on balls, eleven of those which were intentional and he was hit-by-pitch on one occasion. He had 38 home runs and 82 RBI, YET, under the 1956 rules, he would not have had enough at-bats to qualify for the AL batting title, because in 1956 bases on balls did not count as plate appearances.

As mentioned earlier, Williams had previously lost the 1954 batting title to Bobby Avila of the Cleveland Indians, although Williams had the higher batting average. Avila hit .341 while Williams hit .345. However, the numerous walks received by Williams did not give him enough at-bats to qualify for the title.

Williams again lost out for the title last season (1955), when Al Kaline of the Detroit Tigers was declared the AL batting champion with a .340 average, while Williams hit .356, but was at-bat only 320 times officially, far short of the legal figure.

Quite probably the personal problems that Williams had in '55 limited his availability in many games therefore he might not have been a legitimate contender to challenge Kaline.

The rule was changed after the 1956 season, no doubt in part, attributed to Ted Williams. Beginning in 1957, the rule was amended to make how many times a batter faced a pitcher the key element. It was declared that a batter needed 3.1 plate appearances for each of his team's games to qualify for the title, and walks and hit-by-pitches counted for a time at-bat.

The fabulous Ted Williams was always known to many as the best hitter who ever lived. It can be difficult to dispute! This is going back a bit, but in 1949 Williams may have had the best season ever of any hitter.

He was named the American League MVP that season despite losing the batting title to George Kell of Detroit. Kell won with a .343 average, and although Williams also was credited with a .343, Kell was at .3429 to Williams' .3427. One more base hit or one less at-bat would have given Williams another batting title.

The numbers Williams put up in 1949 were similar to many other seasons, but this one was superb. He played in 155 games, had 730 plate appearances, with 566 official at-bats. He had 194 hits, scored 150 runs, with 39 doubles, 43 home runs and 159 RBI's. However, these numbers become even more incredible due to the fact he received 162 bases on balls. Teams would just not pitch to him in close game situations.

In his nineteen year career, most often recognized as the greatest hitter who ever lived Ted Williams received over 2,000 bases on balls, and never had 200 hits in a season, because he was walked so often.

Williams won two Triple Crowns and if not for the afore-mentioned percentage loss to George Kell for the batting title, he would have won a third, a feat that no one has ever accomplished. He finished his playing career with a .344 life-time batting average, 521 home runs and a .482 on-base percentage, the highest of all time.

There were several other seasons when many baseball people felt that Williams should have received the AL MVP award.

Williams was a nineteen time All-Star, a six time AL batting champion and he no doubt would have set records that would never be equaled, except that he served two separate mandatory stints in the military during the peak years of his career.

Ted Williams was the last major leaguer to hit .400, as he accomplished the feat in 1941 with a .406 average.

Most of the young American and National League leaders in the'56 campaign were beginning their journey on the way to Cooperstown and their own ticket to Baseball's Hall of Fame. There were no less than EIGHT rookies during the '56 campaign that eventually became Hall of Famers. The list is comprised of Luis Aparicio, Frank Robinson, Bill Mazeroski, Don Drysdale, Whitey Herzog, Harmon Killebrew, Tommy LaSorda and Sandy Koufax. Add 22 year old Hank Aaron and 21 year old Al Kaline, and it is not difficult to see why this writer refers to the '56 campaign as, "Baseball's Golden Season."

Undoubtedly, the remarkable effort by Don Larsen in Game Five of the 1956 World Series will forever be one of the more memorable events in baseball history.

Perhaps Don Larsen is the best example that sports has to offer of someone who rises from mediocracy to greatness, if even for just one eventful day. While pitching for seven different teams during his fifteen year major league career that ran from 1953 to 1967, the big right-hander posted a career record of only 81-91. He made his major league debut on April 18, 1953 pitching for the lowly St. Louis Browns, who the following season were relocated to Baltimore and became the Orioles. In '54 Larsen had the most losses of any pitcher in all of Major League Baseball as he had a 3-21 record with the Orioles club that lost 100 games. Always a good hitter, Don Larsen set a major league record with seven consecutive base hits.

His World Series masterpiece is most likely the one baseball record that will never be duplicated. The name Don Larsen will forever resonate anytime a pitcher in post season play throws even a few innings of perfect baseball. In short, Larsen made himself the most astonishing hero baseball has ever seen while playing in the 1956 World Series, putting his own exclamation mark on "Baseball's Golden Season."

A resounding bombshell fell on the baseball world on January 14, 1957 as the Major League Baseball career of Jackie Robinson came to an end. He penned a letter to National League president Warren Giles stating that he would retire rather than accept the December 13, 1956 trade to the hated Giants in exchange for pitcher Dick Littlefield. His illustrious and controversial ten year career, all as a Brooklyn Dodger, as well as a civil rights pioneer had changed baseball forever.

In 1947, he had become the first African-American player to appear in a Major League Baseball game. During his career he was National League Most Valuable Player (1949), NL Rookie of the Year (1947), and was a six time All-Star and had a .311 career batting average. His style of daring base running had never before been seen in Major League Baseball.

Robinson helped lead the Dodgers to six World Series appearances. His retirement letter stated that "my retirement has nothing to do with my trade to the Giants organization."

Whether the rivalry was Giants-Dodgers, Yankees-Giants, or Dodgers-Yankees, Major League Baseball was the beneficiary of Baseball's Golden Season!